DARLING MR LONDON

A Farce

ANTHONY MARRIOTT
and
BOB GRANT

SAMUEL FRENCH

LONDON
NEW YORK SYDNEY TORONTO HOLLYWOOD

Copyright © 1978 by Anthony Marriott and Bob Grant
All Rights Reserved

DARLING MR LONDON is fully protected under the copyright laws of the British Commonwealth, including Canada, the United States of America, and all other countries of the Copyright Union. All rights, including professional and amateur stage productions, recitation, lecturing, public reading, motion picture, radio broadcasting, television and the rights of translation into foreign languages are strictly reserved.

ISBN 978-0-573-11113-6

www.samuelfrench-london.co.uk

www.samuelfrench.com

FOR AMATEUR PRODUCTION ENQUIRIES

UNITED KINGDOM AND WORLD EXCLUDING NORTH AMERICA

plays@SamuelFrench-London.co.uk

020 7255 4302/01

Each title is subject to availability from Samuel French,
depending upon country of performance.

CAUTION: Professional and amateur producers are hereby warned that DARLING MR LONDON is subject to a licensing fee. Publication of this play does not imply availability for performance. Both amateurs and professionals considering a production are strongly advised to apply to the appropriate agent before starting rehearsals, advertising, or booking a theatre. A licensing fee must be paid whether the title is presented for charity or gain and whether or not admission is charged.

The professional rights in this play are controlled by Samuel French Ltd, 52 Fitzroy Street, London, W1T 5JR.

No one shall make any changes in this title for the purpose of production. No part of this book may be reproduced, stored in a retrieval system, or transmitted in any form, by any means, now known or yet to be invented, including mechanical, electronic, photocopying, recording, videotaping, or otherwise, without the prior written permission of the publisher. No one shall upload this title, or part of this title, to any social media websites.

The right of ANTHONY MARRIOTT and BOB GRANT to be identified as author(s) of this work has been asserted by them in accordance with Section 77 of the Copyright, Designs and Patents Act 1988.

DARLING MR LONDON

First produced at the Forum Theatre, Billingham
on 7th March 1975
with the following cast of characters:

Edward Hawkins	David Jason
Rose Hawkins	Doreen Keogh
Gordon Routledge	Derek Newark
Mark Thomson	Bob Grant
Mrs Routledge	Rose Hill
Monique	Valerie Leon
Sylvana	Janet Edis
Ingrid	Leena Skoog
Snowdrop	Veronica Barbieri

Directed by Anthony Wiles

Setting by John Page

The action takes place in the living-room of Edward's semi-detached bungalow in Chiswick

Act I An evening in spring
Act II A few moments later

Time—the present

COPYRIGHT INFORMATION

(See also page ii)

This play is fully protected under the Copyright Laws of the British Commonwealth of Nations, the United States of America and all countries of the Berne and Universal Copyright Conventions.

All rights including Stage, Motion Picture, Radio, Television, Public Reading, and Translation into Foreign Languages, are strictly reserved.

No part of this publication may lawfully be reproduced in ANY form or by any means—photocopying, typescript, recording (including video-recording), manuscript, electronic, mechanical, or otherwise—or be transmitted or stored in a retrieval system, without prior permission.

Licences for amateur performances are issued subject to the understanding that it shall be made clear in all advertising matter that the audience will witness an amateur performance; that the names of the authors of the plays shall be included on all programmes; and that the integrity of the authors' work will be preserved.

The Royalty Fee is subject to contract and subject to variation at the sole discretion of Samuel French Ltd.

In Theatres or Halls seating Four Hundred or more the fee will be subject to negotiation.

In Territories Overseas the fee quoted above may not apply. A fee will be quoted on application to our local authorized agent, or if there is no such agent, on application to Samuel French Ltd, London.

VIDEO-RECORDING OF AMATEUR PRODUCTIONS

Please note that the copyright laws governing video-recording are extremely complex and that it should not be assumed that any play may be video-recorded for whatever purpose without first obtaining the permission of the appropriate agents. The fact that a play is published by Samuel French Ltd does not indicate that video rights are available or that Samuel French Ltd controls such rights.

ACT I

The living-room of Edward's detached bungalow in Chiswick. Evening in spring

The room is well, but not expensively furnished, and extremely neat and tidy. Doors lead from it to the spare bedroom, the entrance hall, the main bedroom, the bathroom and the lodger's bedroom. There is also a swing door to the kitchen. At the back is a curtained sun loggia with french windows leading out to a well-kept garden. The room is furnished with a Put-U-Up, a sideboard with a telephone on it, a television set, an armchair, and a couple of small tables. Around the room are various war relics. There is a centre counter-weighted chandelier, which can be pulled down for cleaning, and matching wall lights

As the CURTAIN *rises, Rose Hawkins is cleaning the chandelier, which is now down, with a feather duster. She is a pretty woman in her thirties, neat, lovable and very house-proud. She is wearing an attractive overall over her dress, and rubber gloves. After a moment there is a loud knock at the front door. Rose gives the chandelier a small tug downwards and it goes up to its normal height. She crosses to the hall door and goes off. The front door is heard opening*

Rose (*off*) Hello, Gordon.
Gordon (*off*) Evening, Rose. (*He comes into the room*)

Gordon Routledge, Rose's brother, is a Supervisor at the Continental Telephone Exchange. He is in his forties, pompous, self-important, and likes a drink

    How's my little sister then?
Rose (*following him*) Not too bad, thank you, Gordon. (*She gives him a kiss*)
Gordon Thought I'd just pop in to see Mother on my way home. (*He sits in the armchair and lights a cigarette*)
Rose That was nice of you, Gordon, but I'm afraid she's gone. (*She takes off her overall and gloves*)
Gordon Gone? Poor old soul. When did it happen?
Rose She went on the half-past five bus. (*She gets an ashtray from the sideboard, and puts it on the table by Gordon*)
Gordon What a way to go.
Rose Yes, she should be home by now.
Gordon Oh, I see what you mean. I thought for a moment ... Well, never mind. I'll give her a ring later. How is she?
Rose The same as usual.
Gordon Yes I know what you mean. Fit as a fiddle and complaining of every disease under the sun.
Rose You know that's not true, Gordon. She's not a well woman.
Gordon Nonsense. Mind you, I don't think it's good for her living in that great big house of hers all on her own.

Rose Yes, I'm very worried about her.
Gordon I keep telling her she should sell up. That place is worth a lot of money, and it's not as though I couldn't do with it—she couldn't do with it. She could easily come and live with you and Edward. I mean she practically does now.
Rose I know, and it's not very fair on Edward. I do think you and Marjorie might have her sometimes.
Gordon Of course, I'd love to. But it's Marjorie you know. Can't stand the sight of her.
Rose Is Edward working late at the Telephone Exchange? He didn't say anything about it this morning.
Gordon No, no, no. He's finishing his shift at the usual time—seven o'clock.
Rose Couldn't you have given him a lift then?
Gordon No, I finished early. You can't expect me to hang about quarter-of-an-hour waiting for him.
Rose Well, he is your brother-in-law, after all.
Gordon That's not the point. The Telephone Manager doesn't like Supervisors giving lifts to Operators, even if they are related.
Rose Well, it's quicker by tube isn't it.
Gordon Exactly. I don't know why I lashed out on that new Jaguar XJSix. Eats up petrol, damned nuisance to park. Still somebody in my position can hardly be seen driving around in a Ford, can they.
Rose Edward was thinking of getting a Ford.
Gordon Yes, very appropriate. Mind you, I don't think your husband'll ever pass his test.
Rose He's only had three goes. He's bound to pass sooner or later.
Gordon Well warn me when he does. I'll keep off the roads. (*He chuckles*)
Rose Oh Gordon, he's not as bad as that. It's just that he finds it hard to concentrate.
Gordon Yes he's always day-dreaming. Does it at work. Only this morning a caller asked for Bangkok and he connected them to the Speaking Clock.
Rose He must have misheard. I'd better syringe his ears out.
Gordon It's not his ears you want to worry about, it's his big mouth. Spends most of his time chatting-up foreign girl operators.
Rose I'm sure he's only being polite to them.
Gordon If that's being polite, I'd hate to hear him when he gets really friendly. Well I'll be off then. I've got a busy night ahead of me with the Miss Europhone Contest.
Rose (*not interested*) Oh yes? What about that sack of potatoes you promised me?
Gordon Oh, they're still in my garage. I'll drop them in later on my way to the airport.
Rose Yes, if you wouldn't mind. I've run out and Edward doesn't like spaghetti.
Gordon Oh you pamper him too much.
Rose I think a wife should pamper her husband.
Gordon You want to tell Marjorie that.
Rose She doesn't have much chance to pamper you. You're never at home.

Act I

Gordon I'm not like Edward you know. I don't spend my spare time sitting at home playing with toy soldiers. I lead a very active social life.
Rose (*pointedly*) Yes, so I've heard.
Gordon Yes, well, you don't want to believe everything you hear, you know. Right, I'd better be off. I'll let myself out.

Gordon goes off to the hall

Rose (*calling after him*) Don't forget the potatoes.
Gordon (*off*) No, I won't.

The front door closes off. Rose empties the ashtray into the wastepaper basket and polishes it with a duster. She then plumps up the cushion in the armchair. The telephone rings. She goes and lifts the receiver

Rose Hello? ... Oh, it's you, Mother. You got home all right then? ... You're not all right ... You're not feeling well? ... What? Your legs have gone all wobbly? ... Now Mother you know I can't come over tonight. I'm expecting Edward home any moment and I've got to get his supper ... Why don't you make yourself a nice cup of Oxo, and go to bed with Agatha Christie ... (*wearily*) You haven't got any Oxo? ... No food in the house at all? ... All right then, I'll bring some things over as soon as Edward gets home. (*She puts the receiver down*)

Rose picks up her overall and gloves and goes towards the kitchen. The front door is heard opening off. She hesitates for a second

That you, Edward dear?
Edward (*off*) Yes, Rose, I'm home.
Rose Oh, good.

Rose continues on into the kitchen. The hall door opens and Edward Hawkins enters. He is a neat, diffident, insignificant man in his late thirties. He is a graduate of the University of Life (Failed)

He takes off his hat and coat and puts them on the armchair. He carries a small parcel which he now unties. He opens the box inside and lifts out a dozen or so toy soldiers fixed to a green board. He puts them on the table beside the Put-U-Up

Edward Come on the Grenadiers. Up boys and at 'em. Right, Boney, prepare to meet your Waterloo!

Rose comes back from the kitchen carrying a shopping basket filled with an assortment of food

Rose Hello, dear, had a good day? (*She proffers her cheek for a kiss*)
Edward Yes thank you. (*He gives her a peck*)

Rose puts the basket on the sideboard, gets a medical case and transfers some things to the basket

Rose Now don't get a lot of mess on the carpet will you, I shampooed it this morning.

Edward It's all right, it's only the wrapping from my new soldiers, Rose. I picked them up from the model shop in my lunch hour.
Rose Oh Edward, you haven't been wasting any more money on those toys have you.
Edward Well it's my only vice, Rose.
Rose Yes, I know it is, dear. And I don't really mind, it's just that I don't like a lot of mess.
Edward (*sincerely*) Don't you worry about a thing, Rose. I wouldn't want to put you to any trouble.
Rose I do think Gordon might have given you a lift home.
Edward You know him. Wouldn't lift a finger for anybody. He's been promising me promotion for years and look where it's got me. I'm still only an Operator.
Rose He did make you a *Senior* Operator.
Edward He only did that because all the others retired.
Rose The trouble with you, Edward, is you're too nice to everybody. You let people walk all over you.

Rose puts the basket on the table by the Put-U-Up. Edward just moves the soldiers in time

Edward No I don't, Rose. I just like to be friendly with everybody.
Rose You're too friendly. Gordon says all you ever do at the Telephone Exchange is chat to foreign girl operators.
Edward I'm only being polite to them.
Rose That's not what Gordon says.
Edward He wants to mind his own business.
Rose You shouldn't speak about my brother like that. Gordon's been very good to us. I mean, he got you a job in his department, and found us this house nice and near to Mother.
Edward Yes, he's got a lot to answer for.
Rose What did you say?
Edward I said I've got a lot to be thankful for.
Rose You certainly have. Don't forget my mother gave us the deposit for the house.
Edward Well she's had her money's worth, she's practically lived here ever since.
Rose Oh don't exaggerate, dear. Well, I mustn't stand here chatting to you all evening. I've got to go to Mother's. She's not at all well. She's got one of her dizzy spells.
Edward (*alarmed*) She's not coming back again, is she? She's only just left us.
Rose No, but I must make sure she's all right. I'm only going to settle her in.
Edward Thank goodness for that. It'll be nice to see a bit of television for a change.
Rose You mustn't blame Mother for being a bit old-fashioned. It's just that she finds some of the programme's rather shocking.
Edward Yes, all we've been able to watch for the last three weeks is the *Epilogue* and *Stars on Sunday*.

Act I

Rose You've no sympathy for my mother, Edward. You know how she suffers with her health.
Edward So does everyone else. Anyway, Dr Evans says there's nothing the matter with her.
Rose What does he know about it. He's only just out of medical school. When he's been at it as long as I have, he'll be able to make a proper diagnosis.
Edward But Rose, you're not a doctor. You're not even a nurse. You've only read a couple of books.
Rose I have read every issue of *Family Doctor* for the last twenty years. (*She starts to put on her coat*)
Edward How long will you be gone this time?
Rose I may have to stay overnight.
Edward Well make sure you're back for tomorrow night.
Rose What's happening tomorrow night?
Edward It's the Miss Europhone Contest. I've managed to get two tickets. I wanted to surprise you.
Rose You have. It's the first I've heard about it. What is it?
Edward It's a competition for all the girls from the international telephone exchanges all over Europe, Miss Paris, Miss Rome, Miss Oslo—all of them.
Rose Well, that does sound exciting, I must say. Listening to them jabbering away in foreign languages all night.
Edward Oh no, it's not like that. They're all the pretty girls. They come on in their bathing suits.
Rose (*laughing*) Now I know why you're so keen to go. Well, I'm certainly not going to that. You'd better give those tickets back.
Edward But I paid Gordon ten pounds for them.
Rose More fool you.

Rose gets her handbag out of chair and puts it on the table. Edward manages to save his soldiers again.

Rose goes into the bathroom and returns with a sponge-bag

Edward Any letters for me today?
Rose There's another one with a Paris postmark. It's on the TV. You're getting a lot of letters from abroad these days. And why can't they use your proper name. Why do they always address them to Mr London?
Edward I told you. They're to do with my war games with my soldiers. This one will be from Mr Paris about the Battle of Waterloo.
Rose Tidy your hat and coat away, please. You know I don't like a lot of litter.
Edward Yes, Rose. What am I to do about the lodger?

Edward gets up and takes his hat and coat to the hall

Rose (*taking a compact out of her handbag and titivating*) Our Mr Thomson is not a lodger—he's a paying guest.

Edward returns

I only took him in as a special favour. As the vicar said to me, he can't have his curate living just anywhere. He wanted to find him a nice home.

Edward You'd do anything for that Vicar. You seem to spend half your life in that church.
Rose It wouldn't do you any harm to come down there once in a while.
Edward I might do that. Then I can see all those flowers out of my greenhouse. No, I think I'll leave it till Harvest Festival, then I can see my vegetables as well.
Rose Don't be silly dear.

She picks up the basket to put in the sponge-bag, and plonks it on top of Edward's soldiers. He is horrified

Edward My first regiment of foot guards. My British Grenadiers. You've squashed them all.
Rose Well I'm sorry, but you shouldn't leave your toys lying about.

She puts the sponge-bag in the basket, does it up, and takes it off the table, revealing the squashed soldiers. Edward goes over to the table to examine the soldiers

Edward They're not toys—they're life-like replicas. I got these specially today, so as I could finish the Battle of Waterloo.
Rose Grown men playing at soldiers.
Edward *(picking up a broken soldier)* I expect Napoleon will win now!

Mark Thomson enters from the hall. He is the local curate. He wears a grey suit, dog collar, hat and coat and bicycle clips. He is carrying a small bunch of flowers and some books

Mark Good evening. What a smashing day.
Rose Hello, Mr Thomson. Finished work have you?
Mark I'm afraid not, Mrs Hawkins. The Vicar can put his feet up and watch television, but a curate's work is never done. I've got to bicycle all the way back to St Luke's for a parish meeting at eight o'clock. And I think I've got a slow puncture in my rear.
Rose It's time you got a new one. It's practically falling apart.
Mark I couldn't afford it I fear, Mrs Hawkins. Not on a curate's stipend. *(He puts his hat and coat on the same chair as Edward used)*
Rose *(going to the armchair and putting her basket down)* I really do think it's time they gave you a parish of your own.
Mark I don't think the Bishop's ever quite forgiven me for losing the choirboys on that day trip to Westminster Abbey. They finished up in Soho. *(He sits in the armchair to take off his clips)*
Rose I'm afraid you'll have to excuse me, Mr Thomson. I've got to go and see my dear mother. Her condition has deteriorated. It's her dizzy spells again.
Mark Oh dear, how most distressing for you. Do you think she would like me to go and see her.
Edward No need for that—she's not passing over—she's just passing out.
Rose Don't be flippant, Edward.
Mark That's all right, Mrs Hawkins. Don't mind me. I like Edward's little jokes.

Act I

Rose Edward, be a dear and put Mr Thomson's hat and coat in the hall.
Mark Thank you, most kind. (*He takes off his bicycle clips*)
Rose I do hope you'll be all right while I'm away.

Edward takes the hat and coat to hall, and returns

Mark Don't you worry about me, Mrs Hawkins. Your husband will keep me on the straight and narrow, won't you, Edward?
Rose Edward, I'll phone you up and let you know how Mother is getting on.
Edward That'll be nice.
Rose (*to Mark*) Please apologize to your fiancée for me. I was so looking forward to meeting her. What time are you expecting her?
Mark It's a bit vague. She's hoping to get here tonight, but of course you know the railways. I often think if British Rail had been in charge of the flight from Egypt, Moses would have ended up on Crete.
Rose Well, I've made the bed up in the spare room for her.
Mark How very kind. I've brought a few flowers.
Rose Oh, how lovely of you.
Mark Yes, I thought I'd put them on the dressing-table for my fiancée.
Rose What a nice idea, very thoughtful. Are you sure you've got enough?
Mark I picked all I could find, but your greenhouse isn't very well stocked at the moment.
Edward It never is on Mondays. Are you sure you wouldn't like to pick a few tomatoes as well?
Mark Thank you, but I tried them and they're not ripe yet.
Rose That's Edward's fault. He put them in far too late this year.
Mark Yes, as you sow, so shall you reap.
Edward I'd like to have the chance.
Rose Come along, Edward, let's have a look at you. Oh dear. (*She tidies his hair and tie, etc. during the following*) Mind you keep the place clean and tidy. Don't leave the sink full of dirty dishes. Put the rubbish out tonight, the dustmen come in the morning. I'd rather you didn't have anyone in, I don't want to find everything out of place when I come back. If I'm not back tonight, mind you Hoover right through in the morning. And don't forget Mr Thomson's supper. I'll give your love to Mother. Good-bye, Edward. (*She proffers her cheek*)

Edward pecks Rose's cheek

Rose exits to the hall

Edward (*disarranging his hair and clothes the moment she goes*) Like some supper?
Mark Oh no, thank you. I had high tea with the Mothers' Union. They seem to think just because I'm a curate and a bachelor, I need feeding up. I don't think I'll ever be able to face a rock cake again.
Edward Must be very hard for you.
Mark Yes, like the rock of ages. You should try swallowing them with a dog collar on. I saw you got another of your Mr London epistles in the mail today, on the TV set there.

Edward (*making light of it, and going to the TV set for his letter*) Yes, yes, my war games, the Battle of Waterloo.
Mark It's always struck me as a bit strange, this Mr London business. Odd little alias.
Edward Nothing like that about it. We all take the name of the place where we live. I mean, we'd never cope with all these foreign names. You see this one's from Mr Paris. (*He takes it out of his pocket and shows it to Mark*)
Mark (*taking it*) Looks more like a woman's handwriting to me.
Edward snatches the letter back and puts it in his pocket
Edward No, he's a man. A big fat Frenchman with a long black beard.
Mark Strange how easily one can be deceived.
Edward (*alarmed*) What?
Mark By handwriting.
Edward Ah well, he's a bit the other way, if you know what I mean.
Mark Oh yes I know what you mean all right. I worked under a vicar like that once, in Wimbledon. One had to be extremely careful disrobing in the vestry. One is at a terrible disadvantage with one's cassock halfway over one's head.
Edward Yes, quite.
Mark Silly of me but I seemed to remember you telling me you referred to your lady telephonists as Miss Paris and Miss West Berlin and so on?
Edward Er, well, yes we do.
Mark And they call you Mr London?
Edward Yes, quite right they do.
Mark So naturally one assumed, when one saw letters addressed to Mr London, they were from the foreign young ladies. Pen-friends, as it were. Silly of one.
Edward Ridiculous. I mean I don't even know them. There's nothing personal, they're just voices.
Mark Glad to hear it. One wouldn't like to think a sheep was straying from the fold and turning into a ram.
Edward Oh no, no, I wouldn't dare. I mean I wouldn't dare to dream of it.
Mark Good man. But if you do find yourself dreaming of it, have a cold shower and a good hard rub down after. Works wonders. Well if you don't mind, I'll go and get my things in order for the Parish meeting. (*He goes to his room, passing the table on his way*) My word there's been a massacre here. Vicious chap, your Mr Paris. That's going to keep the padré busy. What was it, artillery and mortar?
Edward No, Rose and her basket.
Mark Never mind. As St Paul said on the road to Damascus: if you can't lick 'em join 'em.

Mark exits to his room, shutting the door

Edward I didn't know St Paul said that. (*He goes to the table, picks up a broken soldier, looks at it sadly, lays it in the box, reverently. Starts to "toot" the*

Act I

Last Post, as he lays another in the box. He closes the box on his finger and cries out)
There is a loud knocking at the front door

Now what's she forgotten?

Edward goes out to the front door and opens it

Monique *(off)* Is your wife home?
Edward *(off)* No.
Monique *(off)* Then perhaps I can come in?

Monique, Miss Paris, sweeps in. She is a gorgeous, chic, French girl, she carries a small case. Edward follows

Edward Yes, of course.
Monique Good, so you got my letter then?
Edward Letter?
Monique And you are alone?
Edward Well—yes.
Monique My darling Mr London.
Edward What did you call me?
Monique Mr London.
Edward Oh, my God! You don't mean—it can't be—you're not ...
Monique But of course. I am Monique, your Miss Paris. You look different from the way you sound. But it does not matter. I promised you a surprise. I have come here to you, my Mr. London, to start the *grande affaire*.
Edward *Grande affaire?*
Monique Yes, we will make passionate love together all night long.
Edward *(reacting as the realization slowly dawns)* I can't! I mean I need my eight hours sleep. I mean I'm not him. I'm not Mr London.
Monique You're not.
Edward I'm not.
Monique But your voice ...
Edward My voice? *(Changing it)* Oh, my voice is quite different. And so am I. He's not like me.
Monique He's not?
Edward No, no, not a bit like me. And I'm even less like him. We could never be mistaken for each other.
Monique But Mr London lives here, he told me so.
Edward No, he doesn't live here, there must be some mistake.
Monique But he gave me his address.
Edward I shouldn't have—he shouldn't have. It must be the wrong address.
Monique He tells me, if ever I come to him before he comes to me, I must write to him first, so he can get rid of his eleventh wife. So I write to him. *(She picks up the letter from the table)* Ah, you have my letter.
Edward Oh! My goodness. I was just going to give it to him, when he comes in.
Monique So he does live here. Why do you tell me he doesn't?
Edward Ah well. I mean he doesn't live here very often.

Monique Ah yes, of course, he is with one of his five mistresses. He is telling me all about them on the telephone.
Edward I was only making it up ... I mean, does he really?
Monique We have such passionate talks on the night-line, *une grande affaire telephonique*! But now we shall be real lovers in the flesh.
Edward Oh my God!
Monique His wife, she has gone?
Edward Yes, but only to her mother's. And he's not here, so you've had a wasted journey. You can go back to Paris.
Monique I cannot do that.
Edward Why not?
Monique I am here for the Miss Europhone Contest. I didn't tell him on the telephone I was coming.
Edward I wish you had, I'd have gone away.
Monique Pardon?
Edward I mean, I'd have gone away and left you together, if he'd been here, which he isn't.
Monique Oh, you are so kind. (*She takes a small perfume spray out of her handbag and sprays herself*) My dear little friend, I think I might have a bit of love to spare for you. (*She gives Edward a quick squirt*)
Edward A bit of spare? My wife wouldn't like that.
Monique Then you should do like him and get rid of her.
Edward Yes, the way things are going I may have to.
Monique We have talked about our affairs so much on the telephone, and now at last we make the final connection.
Edward The final connection?
Monique I cannot wait any longer. I am heating up. Soon I will boil over.
Edward Well, you can't boil over here. She's just shampooed the carpet.
Monique I must see him.
Edward You can't. He's not here. He's gone away. Right away. That's it, he told me he was going to Paris to find you.
Monique Paris?
Edward Yes, he couldn't wait any longer either. There's no point in you staying here, because he's not here, he's there, and you're here not there, and that's neither here nor there because he doesn't know you're here, but you know he's there, so you go there before he gets there and finds you not there and comes back here.
Monique I do not understand.
Edward Neither do I. But don't make me repeat it.

There is a loud knocking at the front door

Monique There's someone at the door. His eleventh wife?
Edward I hope not! Ssh! Pretend we're not here.
Gordon (*off*) Hello, hello! It's me, Gordon.
Edward (*in a panic*) It's Gordon! It's Gordon!
Monique Ah, he is Mr London?
Edward (*loud*) No! Ssh! (*He whispers*) He's my brother-in-law and he mustn't see you. Quick go in there.

Act I

Edward pushes Monique into the spare room, remembers her suitcase, puts it in there, shuts the spare room door

More knocking

Gordon (*off*) Edward, open this door at once. Stop messing about.

Edward goes off, and opens the front door. Gordon enters, followed by Edward

Took your time. Well, where is she?

Edward She? Er—who do you mean?

Gordon Well, Rose, of course, who else? There aren't any other women in the house, are there?

Edward No, no, of course not.

Gordon Well then, where is she? Slaving in the kitchen as usual? (*He goes towards the kitchen door*)

Edward sees Monique's handbag on the table, snatches it up and hides it behind his back

I don't know why she's so good to you. (*He opens the kitchen door*)

Edward She's gone to your mother's.

Gordon Oh, left you at last, has she? Sensible girl. You could get the sack over that.

Edward No, she's coming back.

Gordon More fool her.

Edward slips the bag behind the cushion on the chair

Edward She's only gone to settle Mother in. She's not well again.

Gordon What's the matter with her this time—unless it's fatal I don't want to know. Aren't you going to offer me a drink? I'll have a Scotch. I've just got time for a large one.

Gordon sits in the armchair. Edward tries to whip the bag away

Edward We've only got Nut Brown Ale or sherry.

Gordon I'd better have a schooner of sherry then. What are you doing?

Edward Just plumping your cushion up. (*He plumps it violently*)

Gordon All right, you've plumped it enough. Oh, by the way, I've got your tickets for the Miss Europhone do tomorrow. (*He gets the tickets from his pocket*)

Edward Rose doesn't want to go. (*He gets the sherry from inside the sideboard and pours a glass*)

Gordon (*returning tickets to his pocket*) What a pity. Never mind, they'll do for the Secretary of the Golf Club. I promised him a couple.

Edward Oh, so I'll get my ten pounds back.

Gordon You can't expect him to pay after all he's done for me. Good gracious, this place smells like a French brothel. (*He sniffs round Edward*) You're not going the other way, are you? (*Hopefully*) You could get the sack over that as well. What is that smell?

Edward It's new furniture polish—a sort of French polish. (*He gives Gordon the sherry*)

Gordon drinks and makes a face

Gordon Where do you keep it, in the sherry bottle? (*He sees the soldiers as he puts his glass down on the table*) Still playing toy soldiers, are you?

The spare room door opens slightly

Edward They're not toys. They're life-like replicas. It's a serious hobby. I'm recreating history.
Gordon You live in a fantasy world, don't you? Look at this room, it's like a blooming war museum. I suppose you've still got the spare room full up with your stuff as well.

Edward sees door is open and quickly shuts it

Edward Yes, that's still got a bit of stuff in it.
Gordon Thought so. Usual shambles I suppose. All you can do is play games.

The spare room door opens again, unseen by Gordon. Edward reacts

Games at home, games at the Telephone Exchange, dreaming about far-off places, romancing about far-off people.
Edward No I don't.
Gordon You think I haven't heard you, but I have. How you love being Mr London.
Edward Well, that's what's laid down in the procedure, isn't it?
Gordon It's not laid down in procedure to chat up female operators, is it?
Edward It's only a bit of fun, to pass away the time. Only a bit of make-believe. It's nothing serious.
Gordon Nothing serious? I don't blame Rose not letting you go to the Contest. Goodness knows what you'd get up to if you met any of them face to face.

The spare room door shuts

What was that?
Edward The door. It does that. The house leans that way.
Gordon Yes, talking about your female operators. That reminds me, there was a message for you from one of them at the Exchange just after you left.
Edward What? It couldn't be, you must have got it wrong.
Gordon Don't tell me I got it wrong. I don't get things wrong. I remember it perfectly. Miss somebody or other (*he thinks*)—Frankfurt—Madrid—Brussels?
Edward Miss Paris?

Monique opens the door

Monique *Oui?*

Edward quickly shuts the door behind him

Gordon What?

Act I

Edward We—we must get this door fixed. It's got a life of its own.
Gordon Or was it Rome? Miss Rome?
Edward Anything to do with babies?
Gordon Babies?
Edward Yes, you know, those things that look like miniature people with bald heads.
Gordon What's babies got to do with you and Miss Rome?
Edward Well Miss Rome wants a lot of them but I don't know what she's talking about. So it couldn't be her.
Gordon No, no, something to do with a sauna bath.
Edward Snowdrop!
Gordon Who?
Edward I mean that'll be Miss Oslo. (*Inventing desperately*) She—er—she thought we could have a sauna bath together—er—a sauna bath might be good for—my broken leg.
Gordon What broken leg? You haven't got a broken leg.
Edward (*remembering*) Oh no, that's Miss West Berlin.
Gordon Miss West Berlin's got a broken leg?
Edward No, I have. Er—I have told her I have—er—told her I have to be careful not to get one, roller skating. She's a champion roller skater.
Gordon Roller skating? Sauna bath? Babies? Broken leg? Are you feeling all right? I don't know what the hell you're talking about.
Edward Thank goodness for that. Er, yes I *have* got a bit of a headache as a matter of fact. I think I've been overdoing it a bit lately.
Gordon If you concentrated on your job a bit more and chatting up female operators a bit less, we'd all be a lot better off. Damned uncomfortable this chair. (*He leans forward*)

Edward whips the handbag out, and puts it behind his back

Edward I expect you want to get off home now, eh, Gordon?
Gordon Home?
Edward Yes, back to the lovely wife.
Gordon What's lovely about Marjorie?
Edward Yes, I see what you mean.
Gordon No, I've got to go and look after these Miss Europhone girls. Talking of Marjorie reminds me, I've got that sack of potatoes I promised Rose. They're in the boot. You can come out and get them. (*He gets up*)
Edward Out?
Gordon Well, I can't bring the car in here, can I?
Edward No, I suppose not. You'd never get it through the door.
Gordon Well, come on then.

Gordon goes out through the hall door

Edward quickly throws the handbag in the sideboard cupboard, with a crash of breaking glasses

Edward follows Gordon off, shutting the hall door. Monique's door opens, she comes out, carrying a bottle of brandy

Monique (*smiling*) So, my Mr London—I do not think you have gone to Paris. (*She looks around, puts the bottle of brandy on the table*) Courage for my little Englishman.

Monique goes into the spare room, carrying her case. Mark comes out of his room, carrying a ledger and a small vase of flowers. He notices the bottle of brandy on the table, puts the vase down and picks up the bottle, examines it curiously. Edward enters, carrying a hundredweight sack of potatoes

Edward I've heard about chips with everything but this is ridiculous. (*He sees Mark*) Oh, hello. Bit of Dutch courage for your parish meeting?
Mark No, it's not mine. I can't afford French cognac, even if it is duty free. (*He puts the bottle down*)
Edward French? Er—you haven't—er—seen anyone, have you?
Mark Seen anyone? Who is there to see?
Edward Exactly. No-one. Yes, well, I'll just put these in the kitchen. (*He goes towards the kitchen*)
Mark (*picking up the vase*) Yes, I must be off to the parish punch-up.
Edward Oh, Harvest Festival, is it?
Mark Hardly, in Lent. Just a little welcome for my fiancée, if she turns up.
Edward What a nice thought.
Mark Yes, I'll just put them in the spare room for her. (*He goes to open the spare room door*)
Edward No! (*He drops the sack*)

Mark opens the door. Edward rushes forward, falls over sack. Monique squeals

Mark I am so sorry. (*He closes door then does a double-take*) Edward, there's a—in the spare room—there's a—a—a ...
Edward Girl?
Mark Yes, a girl.
Edward Oh—yes—a girl. In the spare room.
Mark What's she doing there?
Edward Doing there? Oh nothing, nothing at all. Just waiting to go.
Mark Edward, I don't want to come the heavy parson, but you're not thinking of—while your wife's away—extramarital relations, are you?
Edward Pardon?
Mark You're not having a bit on the side?
Edward Oh, those sort of marital relations. No she's the other sort of marital relation, a relation by marriage. My wife's sister.
Mark But your wife hasn't got a sister.
Edward So she hasn't. Of course she hasn't. Ah, she just treats my wife as a sister, but she isn't because she's her sister-in-law. My wife's brother's wife. Have you met Gordon's wife?
Mark No, I haven't.
Edward She's Gordon's wife. Mon ... er—Marjorie.
Mark You mean that girl in there is Gordon's wife.
Edward Yes.
Mark She must be Mrs Routledge.
Edward She must? Yes, she must. I must remember to tell her.

Act I

Mark Surely she knows.
Edward Oh yes, but she's doesn't know he isn't here, because she wasn't here when he went.
Mark Oh I see. I had no idea Mr Routledge had such a young wife.
Edward Neither had he.
Mark I beg your pardon?
Edward I mean, he hasn't seen her yet.
Mark Hasn't seen her yet?
Edward Hasn't seen her clearly yet, because since the day they got married, he's been drunk.
Mark How terrible, poor man. An alcoholic. Can't A.A. help?
Edward There's nothing wrong with his car. It's him.
Mark But what's she doing here?
Edward Ah well, she's run away from him again because he beats her up. Especially when he's on the brandy. So she just grabbed the bottle and ran.
Mark What a terrible story.
Edward I thought it was quite good on the spur of the moment. Oh, I see what you mean.
Mark I can't understand how Mr Routledge manages to hold down such a responsible position at the Telephone Exchange if he's drunk all the time.
Edward Ah, that's just it, you see. No-one knows. It doesn't show. He's very good at hiding it.
Mark How does he manage that?
Edward (*taking the bottle in his hand*) He puts it in the cistern in the staff toilet.
Mark Shall I phone your wife?
Edward Phone my wife? What for?
Mark We should tell her the poor girl's taken refuge here.
Edward Don't do that, she'll go mad.
Mark There's no reason for her to be angry.
Edward Not angry mad, mad mad. It runs in the family. She can't face up to it, you see. It drives her round the bend. The doctor says we must never talk to her about it.
Mark Oh well, in that case I won't say a word.
Edward Good. Now you go to your meeting and I'll get rid of the bird— I mean the burden the poor girl's got to carry.
Mark If you're sure there's nothing I can do?
Edward You've done quite enough already. And I'm very grateful.
Mark Don't thank me. Your wife should be thanking you. I only hope one day she finds out exactly what you're doing.

Mark goes out to the hall

Edward I hope she doesn't. (*He picks up the potatoes*) Why can't we go back to Smash. (*He puts them in the kitchen, then gets the handbag out of the sideboard, puts it on the chair, goes to the spare-room door, bangs on it*) Come on, out! *Allez!* You'll have to go!

Monique comes out

Monique Who was that man?

Edward He lives here. He's the lodger. And what's worse he's a curate.
Monique Curate—what is that?
Edward It's half a vicar, isn't it?
Monique He is half a man?
Edward I don't know. We haven't got time to go into his private life. We've got to get you off to Paris.
Monique (*teasing*) Oh yes, I am going to Paris to meet my lover.
Edward Yes that's it, so we've got to hurry up.
Monique What is the hurry?
Edward You want to catch up with him, don't you?
Monique But I already have. You are here.
Edward Yes, I'm here—but I'm not Mr London
Monique Oh yes, you are. You have teased me long enough. The door was open and I hid behind it.
Edward Oh no!
Monique Yes. I heard everything you said to that nasty man with a loud voice.
Edward That was Gordon. Now what am I going to do?
Monique I will tell you. I'll go in there and get ready, then you will know what to do.
Edward But you mustn't—you can't. I mean I'd like to—but I mustn't.

The telephone rings

Monique goes into the spare room, starting to undress as she goes, and leaving the door open

Edward dithers for a moment, then goes to answer the telephone

Hello ... Oh hello, Rose. Where are you? ... Oh yes, at Mother's. Thank goodness for that. I mean thank goodness that Mother has got you to look after her.

Monique comes on, half undressed

Monique Don't be long.

Monique goes off, removing her bra

Edward sees her off, with a double-take. He is torn between speaking on the phone, and wanting to look at Monique through the bedroom door

Edward Sorry, Rose. I was just looking at the bird—looking at the birds on the lawn. The tits—the blue tits. (*He tries to see more of Monique*) Yes, Rose ... No, Rose ... Yes, Rose ... Yes, Rose ... I mean no, Rose. (*He is now transfixed by what he sees in the bedroom*)

The door closes. Edward slowly turns front, grabs the bottle of brandy and swigs. A moment's pause, then he chokes violently—losing his voice. He speaks in a hoarse gasp

It's all right, Rose. Think I've got a bit of a cold coming on ... Yes, I'll take some aspirin and go straight to bed.

Monique comes out of the bedroom wearing a flimsy négligé

Act I   17

Monique Oh yes, straight to bed. (*She comes close to him*)
Edward Ahh! You ... (*Into the phone*) It's all right, Rose, I was just going atchoo! Good-bye, Rose. No, I won't forget to pay the milkman. (*He slams down the phone*)
Monique There is something wrong. It is too much.
Edward Too much—it's not nearly enough. You can't go parading round here like that. Take it off at once.
Monique Usually that comes later—but, if you insist. (*She starts to undo buttons*)
Edward No, no. (*He rushes to stop her—then whips his hands away as he realizes he is about to touch her*) Ooh! Ah! I mean someone might come in.

There is a knock at the front door

Someone is coming in. Quick, in there, and put your clothes on.
Monique So we can go away together?
Edward Yes, yes, anything you say.

Edward pushes Monique into the spare room then goes to the hall

(*As he goes*) That milkman gets later every morning.
Gordon (*off*) All that nonsense messing about with potatoes ...

Gordon enters

You made me forget my briefcase.
Edward (*off*) You stay here. I'll find it. It was here somewhere.

Edward follows Gordon in

Ah. (*He sits in the armchair before Gordon can, to hide the handbag, and plumps the cushion*)
Gordon (*bellowing*) Edward. Don't sit there poking your cushion. I want my briefcase. There I was standing in the middle of the Skyline Hotel, without it. I looked an absolute fool.
Edward That shouldn't be difficult for you.
Gordon What did you say?
Edward That must've been difficult for you.
Gordon Difficult. It was downright embarrassing—especially in front of all those girls. (*He paces towards the spare room*)
Edward Girls? (*He rises and sits*)
Gordon (*pacing*) Yes, you idiot. All the contestants.
Edward Contestants? (*He rises and sits*)
Gordon The Miss Europhones.

Edward kicks the cushion away by mistake

I've never seen such a bevy of beauties.

Gordon looks away. Edward runs and picks up the cushion. Gordon turns back, Edward dives full length and just manages to cover bag with cushion

Edward Ah!

18   Darling Mr London

Gordon Edward, what on earth are you doing?
Edward Practising for the swimming gala.
Gordon They're a big responsibility—all those lovely girls.
Edward They must be.
Gordon What do you know about it?
Edward Nothing. (*He wriggles desperately, hooking with his foot and hiding the bag*)
Gordon No you couldn't possibly cope with one, could you?
Edward No, I can't—couldn't. (*He rises and moves to spare room door*)
Gordon I'm the only one on that committee who has any idea of organization. Do you know they hadn't even thought of taking a roll call.
Edward Roll call?
Gordon Yes, I'm going back to do it now.
Edward Now?
Gordon Yes. Can't be too careful, one of the girls might be abducted.
Edward Roll call! Abduction. Oh, I could go to prison.
Gordon I'm under a shocking strain you know. Yes I'd better have a decent drink before I go. (*He indicates the brandy bottle and sits in the armchair*)

Mark enters from the hallway carrying an account book

Mark Excuse me. Got the right ledger—wrong year. (*He sees Gordon, addresses him frostily*) Good evening, Routledge.

Mark exits into his room

Gordon Hello, Padré. Lost any more choir boys today, eh? (*He laughs*)

Mark emerges with another ledger

Mark It's all very well to mock, Routledge.
Gordon You're supposed to save souls, not lose 'em.
Mark You may need my help sooner than you think.
Gordon At the moment I'd be grateful if somebody would help me to a drink—Edward? (*He hands Edward the bottle*)
Edward Oh yes, of course.
Gordon Those potatoes were filthy. I'll just wash my hands.

Gordon rises and goes to the bathroom

Mark Edward, do you really think you should.
Edward Eh? Beg your pardon?
Mark Do you think you should, in view of what we were talking about earlier?
Edward Talking about?
Mark Yes, his drinking habits.
Edward Oh, those.
Mark Don't forget about his wife in the spare room.
Edward How could I forget.
Mark We don't want him going berserk, and beating her up.
Edward Well, I don't suppose one little drink will hurt.
Mark He doesn't look too bad at the moment. Just make it a very small one.

Gordon enters

Act I 19

Gordon Right where's my drink? I'm gasping.
Mark Yes, but it doesn't stop at one, does it?
Gordon In this house, seems you're lucky to get *that*!
Edward (*going to the sideboard*) What will you have, another sherry?
Gordon I want to drink, not French polish my liver. I'll have a brandy.
Mark I suppose we can't stop you, as it came from your house.
Gordon *My* house?
Mark Your wife brought it.
Gordon My wife?
Edward (*shutting the sideboard door on his finger*) Ah! Yes, for medical purposes. Thought it might be good for Mother, but she was too late, Rose had gone.
Gordon What on earth did Marjorie want to do that for? She had no right to give my brandy away.
Mark She was only trying to help you to help yourself.
Gordon I can see I shall have to. If I may say so, Padré, that's the first sensible thing you've said since you came in.. Edward, are you going to get me a glass—or have I got to drink it out of the bottle?

Edward goes back to the sideboard

Mark Out of the bottle. He's getting worse.
Edward Just a small one. (*Edward takes a broken glass out, all stem, very little bowl)*

Monique, in bra and slacks, comes out of spare room, sees Mark and Gordon, who have their backs to her. She goes straight back in

Edward No! No! (*He gives the glass to Gordon, and pours brandy into it. It goes on the floor*)
Gordon What do you mean, no?
Edward No, no more than a small one.
Gordon Small? It's non-existent. I'm never going to get a decent drink here.
Mark Just as well. It's your poor wife, we feel sorry for, don't we, Edward?
Edward Er, yes ...
Gordon So you should. Pinching my booze. I'll give her hell when she gets home.
Mark Edward, I really don't think we can stand by and let this happen.
Edward Can't we? I'll go, then.
Mark No, come back. Now, Routledge, old chap. I want you to think of her—a young attractive girl.
Gordon Delighted. Got any particular girl in mind?
Mark Your wife of course.
Gordon What do you want me to do? Think of a young attractive girl or my wife? Make up your mind.
Mark Your wife *is* a young and attractive girl.
Gordon Young and attractive—my wife?
Mark Of course she is, isn't she, Edward?
Edward (*to Mark*) Oh yes, beautiful. (*To Gordon*) Ugly as sin.
Mark So youthful and sweet.

Edward (*to Mark*) Delightful. (*To Gordon*) Tough as old boots.
Mark A lovely young thing!
Edward (*to Mark*) Pretty as a picture. (*To Gordon*) A horror picture. (*Lamely*) Well, after all, beauty is in the eye of the beholder.
Gordon I don't know what the pair of you are talking about. I think I will have a drink after all.

Gordon reaches for the bottle. Mark snatches it up and goes towards the hall door

Mark No, no. I won't let you. I'm taking this with me. I'm going to hide it.
Gordon What do you think you're doing? That's my brandy.
Mark I'm only just beginning, Routledge. This isn't the first time I've done it. I used to get plenty of it in my last parish.

Mark goes out to the hall

Gordon Looks as though he's getting plenty of it here as well.
Edward Plenty of what?
Gordon It's obvious isn't it? The man's on the bottle. He'll be out of his mind by the time he goes into that meeting—if he ever gets that far.
Edward I don't think it's like that.
Gordon It's written all over his face. You'll probably find bottles hidden all over the house. They even hide them in the cistern, you know.
Edward In the cistern, oh, really!
Gordon We'd better search the house right now, before he comes back. Anyway I could do with a drink. You take his room. I'll take the spare room. I bet I'll find something in there.

Gordon goes to the spare room door, Edward bars his way

Edward No!
Gordon What do you mean "no"!
Edward No need. I've already searched. Cleared all the bottles out just before you came.
Gordon Oh, good. (*He sits*) Where did you hide them?
Edward I didn't. I emptied them down the sink.
Gordon That was a stupid thing to do. If I'm not going to get a drink I might as well go. I've still got work to do. I'm going down the road, to the Skyline Hotel, straight to the bar, where there aren't any half-canned curates and half-witted brothers-in-law, and I can get a decent drink in a whole glass. This chair's damned uncomfortable. (*He finds the handbag*) Oh, I was right, you have gone the other way. (*He hands it to Edward*)

Gordon strides out to the hall. The front door slams

Edward notices the briefcase which Gordon has still left behind

Edward Gordon, you've forgotten your—oh-oh. (*He runs to the spare room door*) Come out, come out!
Monique (*off*) Pardon?

Act I

Edward *Venez ici, venez ici!*

Monique comes out. She is still dressed in bra and slacks

Monique You must 'elp me.
Edward What's the trouble? (*He sees her*) Oh no! Why aren't you dressed?
Monique *Le* zip, he is stuck. He will not go up.
Edward If you don't hurry the balloon'll go up. (*He gives her the handbag*)
Monique I cannot go like this, with my trousers, how you say, at half-mast. I will hold it, you pull it.
Edward What?!
Monique The zip.
Edward Oh yes, of course. (*He dithers, torn between the urgency of the situation and his reluctance to touch her*) Oh ... (*Eventually he gives it a mammoth heave, catches his finger in the zip*) Ow! It's got me! I can't get my finger out! Thank goodness my wife can't see me.

The front door is heard to open

Rose (*off*) Edward, where are you?
Edward It's my wife. Get in there, quick! (*He pushes Monique into the spare room—his finger is still caught. He is half-pulled off with her*) Ow! (*He frees his finger*)

Monique exits and closes the spare room door

Edward nurses his finger and sucks it

Rose enters from the hall

Rose Didn't you hear me, Edward?
Edward Good heavens, Rose, what a surprise. You're back soon. Mother better?

Mrs Routledge enters. She is a formidable woman in her late fifties, narrow-minded and anti-permissive

Mrs Routledge No, I'm worse.
Edward Oh, you're here too.
Mrs Routledge No thanks to you. I was forced to travel by public transport. Still, what can one expect from a son-in-law who can't even pass his driving test.

Gordon enters, carrying two cases

Gordon Come on, Edward, give me a hand with these.
Edward You as well?
Gordon I was just getting in the car when they got off the bus.
Edward Oh, isn't that nice. We've got the whole family here now. (*He sucks his finger*)
Rose Edward, why are you sucking your finger. What's the matter with it?
Edward I caught it in the zip—*my* zip—er—you know, in the bathroom.
Mrs Routledge Bathroom? That's what I want. Out of my way.

Mrs Routledge goes into the bathroom, closing the door

Rose It was the journey coming here. It must have upset her.
Edward Well, it's certainly upset me. Why have you brought her back here?
Rose I thought I'd better, now that I've got to give both of you medical attention. How are you?
Edward Very well, thank you.
Rose What about your cold?
Edward What cold?
Rose You told me on the phone you'd got a terrible cold.
Edward Oh, that cold. It's gone.
Rose Don't be silly, dear. You only caught it half-an-hour ago.
Edward Must have been a half-hour cold.
Gordon Rubbish! There's no such thing.
Rose (*feeling his forehead*) You've got a fever, you're delirious.
Gordon Yes, he was behaving very oddly when I was here before. I think he's going peculiar.
Rose I'll give you some of Mother's tablets. They're double strength. That'll get rid of it.
Gordon Tell you what, Rose, give him the bottle full, that'll get rid of him. (*He laughs*)
Edward I'm not having any tablets.
Rose Yes you are. They make Mother feel much better.

Mrs Routledge enters from bathroom

Mrs Routledge I'm feeling worse now. Really dizzy.
Rose Yes, that'll be the tablets. It's quite normal. You'll get used to it. Go and have a lie down.
Mrs Routledge Yes, I think I will.
Edward Yes I should.
Gordon Nothing like a nice lie down.
Rose You can have the spare room, Mother, as usual. It's nice and quiet in there.
Gordon Yes, you have the spare room, Mother.
Edward Yes, it's nice and quiet in there. (*He realizes*) No! I've just remembered. It's *not* quiet in there. In fact it's very noisy.
Rose It's the quietest room in the house.
Edward Not now, it isn't.
Mrs Routledge What are you talking about, Edward?
Edward It's the planes from Heathrow Airport. They fly right over the spare room now.
Rose You *are* delirious.
Mrs Routledge He's talking gibberish.
Gordon I told you he was going peculiar.
Mrs Routledge He's not safe. He ought to be put away. I'm going to lie down in the spare room, *and* I'm going to lock my door.
Edward No, you can't go in there, it's being used. I mean, I've been using it. I've got all my soldiers out. And my fort. I'm fighting the Hundred Years' War, and I've only just started the first year.

Act I

Mrs Routledge Well you'd better get rid of your toys at once before I put them in the dustbin.
Rose Yes, Edward, do move them. Mother must have the spare room. You sit down here, Mother. I'll make a nice cup of tea. You want a cup, Gordon?

Rose goes off to the kitchen

Gordon No, I want something stronger. Anyway I've got to get over to the hotel. Make sure all those girls are safe and sound. Good night, Mother. Good night, Edward—or should I say Edwina. (*He laughs*)

Gordon goes out to the hall; the front door slams

Edward Well, I'll clear out the spare room for you, Mother. (*He does not move*)
Mrs Routledge Well, go on then. And hurry up about it. (*She looks round*) What have you done with my handbag? It's got my tablets in it.
Edward You must have left it in the bathroom.

Rose puts her head out of the kitchen door

Rose Tea's just brewing. (*To Edward*) Haven't you cleared that room yet?
Mrs Routledge No, he hasn't. I'm just going to take my tablets, Rose.

Mrs Routledge goes into the bathroom

Rose That's right, Mother. Do hurry up, Edward.

Rose disappears

Edward shuts the bathroom door, produces a key from behind his back, and locks the door. He catches his tie in the door and has difficulty trying to get it out. Eventually he goes and opens the spare room door

Edward (*whispering*) Quickly!

Monique comes out in bra and pants

Oh no, why aren't you dressed?
Monique (*normally*) *Le* zip is completely broken.
Edward Ssh! My wife's back.
Monique She will come between us.
Edward Yes, with a meat axe. In here quick.

Edward bundles Monique into Mark's room, shuts the door and moves o

Monique (*opening the door*) My clothes.
Edward Ssh! I'll get them. (*He gives her the key*) Lock yourself in. Don't open the door unless I knock.

Edward pushes her back in, runs to the spare room, and goes in. Rose comes out of kitchen with two cups of tea, puts them on the table, with her back to the spare room. Edward comes out of the spare room with Monique's overnight case, sees Rose, hides it behind his back

Rose Have you done it all?
Edward Nearly. (*He backs to the door of the main bedroom, opens it, throws the case in, closes the door*) That's the lot.

Rose Where's Mother?
Edward In the bathroom.
Mrs Routledge (*off, banging on the door*) Open this door.
Rose Just turn the key, Mother.
Mrs Routledge (*off*) I can't. It's gone.
Rose It can't have gone. Look on the floor, it must have dropped out.
Mrs Routledge (*off*) No, it hasn't. It's been taken away.
Rose Don't be silly, Mother. Who'd want to do a thing like that? (*Accusing*) Edward!
Edward It wasn't me. The door must have jammed. The house is subsiding.
Mrs Routledge (*off, shouting*) Let me out!
Rose Don't just stand there, let my mother out.
Edward I'll have to break the door down.
Rose You can't do that.
Mrs Routledge (*off*) Help! Help! Murder! Police!

There is a knock on the front door

Rose (*to Edward*) Now see what you've done. That's probably the police.

Rose exists to the hall. Monique opens her door

Monique I heard the knocking. Is it time for us to go now?
Edward No. No. Get back in and keep the door locked.

Monique disappears

Mrs Routledge (*off*) Somebody get the fire brigade.

Gordon and Rose enter

Edward You'll have to climb out of the window, Mother.
Rose Don't be silly. She could break her neck.
Edward Some hopes!
Gordon You've gone too far this time, Edward. We'll have to break the door down. Out of the way. This is a man's job. (*He lunges at the door. It does not budge, and he clutches his shoulder in agony*) Edward, break the door down.

Edward takes a run at the door, hits it, it flies open and he falls inside, out of sight. A big crash. Edward staggers out with the plastic lavatory seat around his neck then staggers back in

Mrs Routledge (*off*) I'm stuck. I'm stuck. Get me down.
Rose Edward, get her down at once. You're trying to kill my mother.
Gordon And you're not making a very good job of it. Grab her legs. You lout, assaulting a poor defenceless old lady.
Mrs Routledge (*off*) Take your hands off my knickers.

Edward comes in with Mrs Routledge on his shoulders

Put me down. He's making away with me.
Rose Put her down, put her down.
Mrs Routledge Don't drop me. I'm delicate.

Act I

Gordon Let go, let go of her.
Edward I'm trying to. She's got me in a Boston crab.

Rose and Gordon tug at Edward trying to get Mother down. But they are not helping. They stagger round the room and collapse in a heap on the Put-U-Up

Mark enters from the hallway. He rushes over to Gordon and drags him clear

Mark Pull yourself together, man. You mustn't go around attacking people like this.
Mrs Routledge He attacked me in the bathroom.
Gordon (*pointing at Edward*) It wasn't me, Mother.
Mark (*humouring him*) Yes, yes, that's what you think now. It'll all seem clearer in the morning. You must remember, moderation in all things.
Gordon Yes. Why don't you practise what you preach?
Mrs Routledge He's violent—like a mad thing.
Mark Don't distress yourself, Mrs Routledge. (*To Gordon*) It's the drink.
Gordon (*to Mark*) Yes, it is the drink.
Mrs Routledge (*pointing to Edward*) I knew it. He's a secret drinker.
Rose Come along, Mother. I'll take you to your room. You must lie down.
Mrs Routledge I've been saying it for years, he should be put away. (*Backing Edward*) People aren't safe with a madman like you around.
Rose Come along, Mother. Don't let him upset you.
Mrs Routledge If I don't get over this, I'll have him charged for murdering me.

Mrs Routledge and Rose go into the spare room

Edward That'll be nice. Well, Gordon, how did you get on at the hotel?
Gordon I didn't. I've just realized I've got a big problem.
Mark Thank goodness you've realized it at last.
Gordon It's about time you realized you've got a problem. I suppose all the brandy's gone?
Mark Yes, it's gone, where you won't find it.
Edward I suppose you'll be going home now?
Gordon Home? Certainly *not*. I'm going back to that hotel. I'm going to lick this problem once and for all—I've had enough of it.
Mark Glad to hear it. That's the spirit.
Gordon Spirit. That's the one thing I haven't had enough of.

Gordon goes, slamming the front door

Mark How disappointing. Just when I thought we were well on the way.
Edward Yes, well, I expect you'll want to be on *your* way.
Mark Yes, I must be getting back to my meeting. They want *last* year's figures now. I'll get the book. (*He goes to his room and tries it, finds it locked*) That's funny, it won't open.
Edward That's right. I gave her the key so it's locked. I mean it's blocked—cocked—cock-eyed—because the house is falling down. Don't worry, I'll fix it later, while you're out. (*He tries to push Mark towards the hall door*)
Mark But I need that book now. Tell you what, I'll go round the back and climb in through the window.

Edward No! I'll go round the back and climb in through the window. I'll be much quicker, vicar.
Mark It's the ledger with the green cover, on the desk.
Edward Right.

Edward goes out through the french windows. Rose comes out of the spare room

Rose Mother's quieter now. I've managed to settle her down.
Mark I do admire you, Mrs Hawkins—you've got so many problems to deal with in your family.
Rose Yes I have. Where's Edward?
Mark He's very kindly climbing through the window of my room to get my book.
Rose Why didn't he go through the door?
Mark It's jammed. The house is falling down you know.
Rose Not that nonsense again. (*She goes to Mark's door and rattles it, then bangs on it)* Edward, what are you doing? Come out of there at once.

Mark and Rose are both at the door with their backs to the sun loggia

Edward and Monique creep in through the french windows. Edward has the book. Monique is still in bra and pants. They go into the main bedroom

Mark I expect he's on his way back.
Rose Don't worry. I'll see he fixes that door before your fiancée gets here, Mr Thomson.
Mark It doesn't look as if she's coming tonight after all, Mrs Hawkins. I fear British Rail must have let her down. I haven't heard any more.
Rose I suppose he's got stuck in the window now. (*She bangs on the door*) Edward! Are you stuck! Edward!

They listen at the door

Edward creeps in from the main bedroom, shuts the door quietly, tip-toes to the hall door, opens it quietly, shuts it noisily

Mark and Rose jump

Edward Here I am.
Rose Oh Edward, you mustn't frighten people like that. What are you doing?
Edward I've just been round the back to fetch his book and now—I've come back round again. Here you are. (*He holds out the book*)
Mark How very kind of you, Edward.
Edward I've fixed up your door, you can open it now.
Mark (*taking the book*) Thank you. I shan't be long. I hope you don't mind but one of my young parishioners telephoned me this morning. She's calling round to discuss her forthcoming marriage. It won't last long.
Edward Why, aren't they well suited?
Rose Edward! Not at all. I think it's so important that young people should know what they're letting themselves in for.

Act I

Edward (*to himself, looking towards the main bedroom*) I wish I'd known what I was letting myself in for.
Mark Mrs Hawkins, I know you don't want to talk about it, but I do want to help you with your problem.
Rose Problem? We haven't got a problem, have we, Edward?
Edward (*weakly*) Speak for yourself.
Mark I don't mean you, Mrs Hawkins, I'm thinking about the poor young girl.
Rose Poor young girl?
Mark Yes, Edward's trying to fight it, but he needs your help.

Mark exits to the hall

Rose Young girl? What young girl? And what are you trying to fight?
Edward I'm not fighting a girl, it's a battle. I'm fighting—er—the Battle of Calais. Joan of Arc and all that.
Rose Oh, you mean your daft war games.

Mrs Routledge enters from the spare room

Mrs Routledge Rose!
Rose What is it, Mother?
Mrs Routledge I am absolutely perished. Bring me a hot-water bottle.
Rose But I gave you the electric blanket, Mother.
Mrs Routledge I don't trust that contraption. Edward's trying to electrify me. I demand a hot-water bottle.
Rose All right, Mother.
Mrs Routledge (*sarcastically*) And in case you've forgotten, it's time for my Oxo.

Mrs Routledge goes back

Rose Yes, all right, Mother.

Rose goes to the kitchen

Edward goes to the main bedroom door, opens it

Edward Come on, quickly, before my wife comes back. (*He carries Monique's case out*)

Rose comes out of the kitchen

Rose Edward!

He shuts the door

Edward, do try not to upset Mother. You can see she's in a terrible state.
Edward She's not the only one!
Rose Whose is that case?
Edward What case? Oh, this case. It's not mine.
Rose I know that, and it's not mine. So whose is it?
Edward Er—Mr Thomson's.
Rose Mr Thomson's? That's a lady's case.

Edward Yes, it's Mr Thomson's lady's case ... I mean it's his fiancée's. That's it. It's his fiancée's.
Rose Oh, she's here?
Edward Is she? I suppose she must be.
Rose I'm looking forward to meeting her.
Edward So am I. I mean she's not stopping. She's just passing through.

Monique enters

Monique I'm ready now. (*She sees Rose*) Oh!
Rose (*aside to Edward*) Edward! Who is that young woman?
Edward Who is that young woman? Er—she's—she's ...
Rose (*realization dawning*) Oh, of course, she's Mr Thomson's fiancée. Why didn't you say so before?
Edward I didn't think of it. I mean, of course she is.
Rose (*going to Monique*) How do you do. I'm so glad you were able to make it after all. You are stupid, Edward, you put her in the wrong room. You must have this room of course. (*She indicates Mark's room*)
Monique C'est très jolie, Vous êtes très aimable, madame. C'est très bon pour l'amour, n'est-ce-pas?
Rose Are you by any chance foreign?
Monique Foreign? No, I am French.
Rose French? Of course. You are daft, Edward, making a mystery of it. All that nonsense about Joan of Arc. (*To Monique*) My husband lives in a world of his own, you know.
Edward I wish I did.
Rose It's so nice to meet you at last. He was so afraid British Rail might have let you down.
Monique Pardon?
Rose He's told me so much about you.
Monique Oh, has he? You do not mind that I take him away from you?
Rose Well, of course I should be sorry to lose him—but I think you're going to be so good for him. When are you thinking of getting married?
Monique Married? Ha, ha, ha!

Edward laughs with her, forcedly

We are going to have *la grande affaire*.
Rose How do you mean, a grand affair?
Edward She means a big do, you know, lots of people.
Monique No, no. It will be just the two of us.
Rose Oh, just a quiet ceremony? What a shame.
Monique You think we should have what you call *le* gang bang?
Rose Gang bang?
Edward Yes, gang bang, er—what she means is—should she get the Boy Scouts to do a firework display at the reception.
Monique Yes, there will be fireworks in the bedroom.
Edward There will be fireworks in here in a minute.
Mrs Routledge (*off*) Rose, will you please hurry up with my hot-water bottle?
Rose Coming, Mother. Excuse me a minute.

Act I

Rose goes off to the kitchen

Monique Who is that?
Edward That's somebody you haven't met, and you're not going to, because she's not very nice when you meet her, which you're not going to do, because you're going. (*He pulls her towards the front door*)
Monique And you are coming with me?
Edward No—well, I mean not yet. I mean you go on ahead.
Monique Where shall I go?
Edward To the hotel. (*He pushes her towards the hall*)
Monique And you will join me later?
Edward Yes, yes. I'll join you later.
Monique A bientôt.
Edward Yes, and you too.

Edward pushes Monique out of the front door. Rose comes in from the kitchen with a hot-water bottle

Rose I was just thinking ... Oh! Edward, where are you?

Edward enters

Edward (*happily*) Here I am, Rose.
Rose Where's she gone?
Edward She's gone, that's where she's gone. She couldn't stay because she had to go. So she went. And she's not coming back. (*He picks up the tea tray*)
Rose What a pity, she seemed such a nice girl. Then you'd expect it of a curate's fiancée.
Edward Oh, yes, yes you would. (*He sits*)
Rose Don't sit down, Edward, the kettle's boiled. Be a dear and make Mother's Oxo.
Edward Yes, Rose. Delighted.

Edward skips off to the kitchen, taking the tea-tray

Rose looks at him suspiciously, then goes towards the spare room

Rose Now you will be careful where you put this, Mother, it's boiling hot.

Rose goes into the spare room. As the spare room door closes the hall door opens, and Mark enters with Monique

Mark Please don't distress yourself, my dear. We're all trying to help you.
Monique No, no. I must go to the hotel.
Mark No, no. You mustn't go to a hotel in your condition. Just leave everything to me.
Monique Oh, very well. (*She sits on the Put-U-Up*)

Mark sits beside her

Edward enters with a cup of Oxo

Edward Here we are, I've got Mother's Ox-oh! My God!

Edward goes back into the kitchen quickly. There is a crash off. Rose comes out of the spare room

Rose Oh! You haven't gone after all. That's nice. Edward, where's Mother's Oxo?

Edward comes in holding the handle of the mug

Edward *(proffering the handle)* Here you are.
Rose Edward! Where's the rest of it?
Edward On the kitchen floor.
Rose What do you expect my mother to do? Get down on all fours and lap it up?
Edward No, it broke. I think I made the Oxo too strong.
Rose Well, clear it up at once, and make some more.

Edward goes

We were talking about the marriage.
Mark Oh, what a sad affair.

Edward darts back

Edward We've run out of Oxo.
Rose Run out? We had five cubes.
Edward I told you I'd made it too strong.
Rose Well, make her some tea. Make us all some tea. Go on.

Rose sits on the armchair, Mark sits beside Monique on the Put-U-Up

Edward goes

What do you mean, Mr Thomson, sad? Monique seems very happy.
Monique Oh, I am very happy.
Mark Yes, yes, just putting a good face on it—very brave girl. *(He goes to pat her knee with his hand, then thinks better of it)*
Rose I think she's a very lucky girl.

Edward shoots in with a tea-trolley on which there is a packet of tea, a packet of sugar, a half-full bottle of milk, teapot and several odd cups, in disorder, and a kettle

Rose What are you doing, Edward?
Edward Making tea.
Rose Have you gone mad?. You can't make tea in here.
Edward I can't make it in there. There's lino on the Oxo, there's Oxo on the crockery, Croxo on the lino—ockery on the croxo—it's very wet in there!
Rose Well, mind you don't make any mess. So I hear you're going to have a big do afterwards?
Monique Ah yes, as soon as we can get to bed. *(She looks at Edward)*

Edward, about to pour the tea out of the packet into the teapot, pours it all into the milk bottle by mistake. He realizes what he has done, and pours the mixture from milk bottle into teapot

Act I

Rose Yes, I believe there's going to be fireworks.
Monique Yes, all through the night.
Rose I understand it's what they call a gang bang.

Edward riveted by the conversation, now has the sugar packet in his hand, over the teapot. He squeezes it convulsively. The bottom bursts and, unseen by him, the sugar pours into the pot. He opens the top of the packet, and goes to tip the sugar into a cup. There is none. He screws up the packet and throws it away

I understand you want to keep it quiet.

Edward starts pouring water from the kettle into the teapot

Mark Naturally, we have to be careful with her drunken husband.
Rose What?
Mark Yes, I knew about the drink and beating her up, but I didn't know about the orgies.
Edward No!

Edward turns in horror from the table, letting water pour on to the carpet. Rose sees him

Rose Edward, what are you doing on my carpet?
Edward Ah yes. (*He quickly starts pouring into the teapot*) Making the tea. It's ready. I'll be mother. (*He tries to pour the tea from the teapot but nothing comes out. He shakes and bangs it—still nothing comes out. He blows down the spout—still nothing happens. He tries to break the spout off—won't break. He pours sludge out of the top of the pot into three cups*)

At this moment Mrs Routledge emerges in her nightie

Mrs Routledge Rose! Do I have to wait all night for one simple cup of Oxo?
Edward I'm afraid there isn't any, Mother. Have a cup of tea instead. Here you are. (*He holds out a cup to Mrs Routledge*)

Mrs Routledge looks at it

Mrs Routledge How dare you! Oh! Oh! I can feel another of my dizzy spells coming on.

Mrs Routledge goes into the spare room

Rose jumps up and goes to the spare room door as it slams in her face

Rose Mother, please let me in. You shouldn't be out of bed. You'll catch your death of cold.
Mrs Routledge (*off*) Yes, that's just what he wants.
Rose (*struggling to open the door*) Mother, will you please open this door.
Edward Get into bed. What a good idea, let's all get into bed, it's late.
Monique Ah, now we have the gang bang.
Edward No, no, no!
Mark But it's only half-past eight.
Edward (*to Monique*) Well, she's tired, aren't you?
Mark Yes, I'm sure you're tired after your ordeal.

Monique No, I'm not a bit tired.
Edward Of course you are. You want to go to bed, don't you.
Monique (*jumping up*) Oh yes, I want to go to bed.
Edward There you are, what did I tell you?
Rose Oh, you must have Mr Thomson's room, of course. I'll get it ready for you. I'll get some clean sheets from the airing cupboard. (*She goes to the bathroom*) Edward, do tidy up that mess.

Rose exits to the bathroom

Mark Poor soul. Drunkenness, beating, gang bangs. You need all the rest you can get. I'll go and get my things out. (*He picks up a vase of flowers*) You must have these flowers. They'll cheer you up.

Mark goes into his room, taking the flowers with him

Monique goes over to Edward and starts to kiss him

Edward Right, we've got to get you out of here.
Monique Now we can start.
Edward No, no. My wife.
Monique But she knows all about us. She says she doesn't mind.
Edward That's what she *says* yes. She's very cunning. She's trying to get evidence.
Monique Evidence?
Edward For a divorce. She's been trying to get one for years, clear me out, take all my money.
Monique She is a wicked woman. She is not a wife, she is more like your old mother.

Rose comes in from the bathroom with the sheets

Rose What did you say, dear?
Edward She said what a lot of life there is in poor old Mother.
Rose Oh, that's nice of you.

Rose goes into Mark's room

Edward You must go at once.
Monique But I can't leave you to her.
Edward (*pushing her to front door*) But you must, you must,

Mark comes out of his room with night things

You must have a look at my hollyhocks.
Mark Good idea, Edward. Nature has a wonderfully calming effect.
Edward Not with her nature, it doesn't.
Mark No sign of my young parishioner. I hope she hasn't got cold feet about her wedding.

Mark goes back into his room

Edward Quick, before it's too late.

There is a loud knocking at the front door

Act I

It is too late, it's Gordon, come for his briefcase. (*He looks round at the rooms*) Quick, in the bathroom.
Monique Why?
Edward He's taken a roll call, he knows you're missing.
Monique Oh, my darling, he will take me from you—put me in that dreadful hotel.
Edward He'll put me in prison.

Renewed knocking

Edward pushes Monique in the bathroom and shuts the door

More knocking

Rose pokes her head out of Mark's room

Rose Edward, there's someone at the door.
Edward Yes, I know, it's only Gordon.

Rose goes back. Edward goes out to the hall and opens the front door, off

Oh, I thought it was somebody else. Go in. He's expecting you.

Sylvana, Miss Rome, enters. She is a fiery Italian. Edward follows her

You've come to see about your wedding?
Sylvana Yes, my wedding.
Edward (*going to Mark's room*) I'll tell him you're here. He's been waiting.
Sylvana He is waiting, my *bella* Mr London.
Edward Mr London! Who the hell are you?
Sylvana I am Miss Roma.
Edward Oh, my God—another one!

Mark enters, carrying the vase of flowers

Mark They need water.

Edward leans on the trolley, it shoots away and he falls. Mark falls over the trolley. The flowers go up in the air and Sylvana catches them. Edward runs into the bathroom as:

the CURTAIN *falls*

ACT II

The same, a few moments later

Sylvana is sitting on the Put-U-Up. Mark is near the bathroom door

Mark Oh dear me. He must have been in a great hurry to go to the bathroom. What are you doing in there, old chap?
Edward (*off, in the bathroom*) I'm not getting in the bath.
Mark Who is this young lady?
Edward (*off*) She's come to see you.
Mark Oh, I see. (*To Sylvana*) Oh, I do beg your pardon. Yes, I was expecting you. Would you like a cup of tea?
Sylvana No thank you.
Mark (*surveying the wreckage on the trolley*) Yes, I think you're very wise. I'll just get rid of these. (*He wheels trolley up and pushes it off into kitchen, then returns*)
Sylvana It is so good to see you at last, in the flesh.
Mark In the flesh?
Sylvana *Si*. I have told my brothers all about you. They cannot wait to come to the wedding.
Mark The wedding. Yes it is rather short notice. Perhaps we'd better get started right away.
Sylvana But of course. That is why I am here. You do not look like you sound.
Mark I beg your pardon?
Sylvana You do not look like you sound on the telephone.
Mark Oh, I see. Yes, the telephone's very deceptive. *You* don't sound like *you* sound on the telephone. So you want to get married.
Sylvana But of course, that is all I want in the world—and many, many babies.
Mark Yes, well, first things first. At least I hope it's first things first.
Sylvana What do you mean?
Mark Well, I mean you haven't—I mean this isn't—well, we're not as it were, closing the stable door, are we?
Sylvana You did not tell me you had any horses.
Mark I haven't.
Sylvana Then why do you need a stable?
Mark No, no. I mean you're not getting married because it is necessary?
Sylvana Yes, it is necessary, to have many babies.
Mark Yes, well, you seem to understand that side of things. Good. When do you want to get married?
Sylvana As soon as possible.
Mark (*consulting his diary*) Yes, well, let's see where we can fit you in, shall we? How about three weeks next Saturday at two-fifteen. That'll give us time to call the banns.

Act II 35

Sylvana Yes, the bands, *la bella musica*, we must have *la musica*.
Mark Of course, Mr Hargreaves will be available on the organ, but we'll come to that later. Where would you like to get married, St Mark's or St Luke's?
Sylvana St Peter's.
Mark I'm afraid we haven't got a St Peter's. They've got one at Ealing, but of course that's not in this parish.
Sylvana No, St Peter's in Rome. You will come there.
Mark Rome? That's definitely not in this parish. Of course it's very flattering of you to ask me, but I'd have to get a special dispensation from Canterbury.
Sylvana Who is he?
Mark The Archbishop.
Sylvana But I don't want Archie Bishop to marry me, I want you to marry me.
Mark Well, in that case, it'll have to be St Mark's or St Luke's.
Sylvana O.K. Whatever you say. I will bring all my family here.
Mark Splendid. I shall look forward to meeting them. If I'm there, of course.
Sylvana But you must be there.
Mark Well, I'll do my best, but I see we have a jumble sale and indoor fete on that day. And I did promise to look after the hoop-la.
Sylvana But how can I get married if you aren't there?
Mark Don't worry. The Vicar'll marry you. He's better at it than me, had more practice.
Sylvana But I don't want this Mr Vicar, I want you. Only you. If you do not marry me, my brothers will kill you. (*She mimes slitting her throat*)
Mark (*nervously*) Oh dear, well, in that case, I think I'll put off the hoop-la. Never makes any money anyway. I really would love to marry you.
Sylvana *Multe bene.* (*She embraces him*) We will make such lovely babies. Many, many babies. Oh *carissimo!* (*She launches herself at him*)

Rose comes out of the spare room

Rose Mr Thomson!
Mark (*jumping up*) Oh, hello, Mrs Hawkins.
Rose What do you think you're doing?
Mark We were just talking about making babies.
Rose Making babies? Not on my Put-U-Up you won't.
Sylvana Yes, yes. We will be making many babies when we are married.
Rose (*to Mark*) You can't marry her.
Mark I've got to, Mrs Hawkins. If I don't her brothers will kill me. (*He mimes slitting his throat*) I offered her the Vicar, but she doesn't want him.
Rose Offered her the Vicar, but what about your fiancée?
Mark She won't mind. I'm hoping she'll run the hoop-la—while I'm doing it.
Sylvana You've got a fiancée?
Mark Of course I have a fiancée.
Sylvana You have a fiancée. *Sporgo indigeno!* My brothers will kill you!
Mark Kill me?
Rose Mr Thomson. I like to think I'm broad-minded, but I cannot have a lodger who is engaged to two young women at the same time, making babies

on my Put-U-Up and getting himself killed all over my carpet. I must ask you to pack your things and leave, and take your harem with you.
Mark But my dear lady ...
Rose Don't you dear lady me. I want nothing more to do with you.

Mrs Routledge comes in from the spare room

Mrs Routledge Out of my way.
Rose Mother, what are you doing?
Mrs Routledge I'm going to the bathroom. That is, if nobody has any objection.
Mark No, no, of course not. The call of nature must be answered.
Mrs Routledge When I want your permission, padre, I'll ask for it. (*She reaches the bathroom door*) It won't open. Who is that in there?
Edward (*off*) Go away, I'm doing something.
Mrs Routledge Come out of there at once.
Rose Edward! Open the door. Mother wants to use the bathroom.
Edward (*off*) She'll have to go down the road to the public toilet.
Mrs Routledge He's trying to do me an injury. I can't wait any longer. Out of my way.

Mrs Routledge dashes out through the hall door, and Rose dashes after her

Rose (*as she goes*) Edward, I'll never forgive you for this. Mother, come back, you can't go out in your nightie.
Mark Mrs Routledge. You haven't got two p. You'll need two p.
Sylvana She called that man in there "Edward".
Mark That's right.
Sylvana But you are Edward.
Mark No, no. I'm not Edward, I'm Mark.
Sylvana Then you are not the one I came to see.
Mark You mean you're not Miss June Phillips of Nineteen, Montrose Avenue?
Sylvana No. I am Sylvana Celli of Roma.
Mark That explains everything. You've got the wrong chap. Edward, there's somebody here to see you. Never mind, when you find the right chap, I'll still be happy to marry you. Now if you'll excuse me, I've just got to go and assist Mrs Routledge with her call of nature. Her cup runneth over, as it were.

Mark goes out through the hall. Edward comes out of the bathroom, quickly, closing the door behind him

Sylvana Oh Edward, my darling Mr London. Why do you run away from your Sylvana? You are not shy, are you?
Edward No, I'm not shy—just petrified!
Sylvana Why do you leave me with this man who wants to marry me with Mr Vicar while his fiancée jumps through the hoop-la.
Edward Take no notice of him. It's the drink—he's been at the *vino*.
Sylvana He is crazy. You do not have a fiancée?
Edward Fiancée—no, no.

Act II

Sylvana Good. If you have another woman—my brothers will kill you. (*She does her throat-slitting mime*)
Edward Another woman—what an idea. (*He feels his throat nervously*)

Taps are heard running in the bathroom

Sylvana What is that?
Edward Oh, my God, she's having a bath.
Sylvana So, you have a girl in there!
Edward No, no, not a girl—a bird—a she bird in the bath. We've got a birdbath in the bathroom, and the bird's bathing in it.

There is a big splash off

Sylvana It must be a big bird.
Edward Big? She's a whopper. She's got a great big—wings. Flaps them about.
Sylvana Oh, I would like to see her.
Edward No, no, you can't, she's dangerous. She's a man-eating bird—she's a vulture.
Sylvana But vultures do not swim.
Edward Or rather not a vulture—more of a swan. Yes, a swan—a mad swan from the desert, where the vultures are.
Sylvana Why is she mad?
Edward What swan wouldn't be mad stuck in the desert with no water, for hundreds of miles. (*He pushes her towards Mark's room*) Quick, you'd better go in here in case she gets out. She doesn't like strangers, only to eat.

Edward bundles Sylvana into Mark's room. Monique comes out of the bathroom, wrapped in a towel

Edward reacts

Ah! What are you doing wandering around dressed like that?
Monique You don't like it on?
Edward No I don't.

Monique starts to undo her towel

Yes I do! I mean I don't know what I mean.

Edward goes into the bathroom

Monique What are you doing? It is time for us to start?

Edward returns

Edward It is time for us to finish. Put your clothes on at once.
Monique Then I must take this off first. You will help me?
Edward No, no, not in here.
Monique All right in here. (*She tries to drag him into the main bedroom*)
Edward No, no.
Rose (*off*) Mother, wait for me ...
Edward Yes, yes.

Monique goes into the main bedroom. Edward goes to follow. She throws the towel out, shouts "voilà!" He reacts in horror as he sees her naked (off) and quickly goes in and slams the door. Mrs Routledge runs in through the hall door, followed by Rose, Mark and Gordon

Mrs Routledge They've no right to close it, it's supposed to be public.

Mrs Routledge dashes into the bathroom and shuts the door

Rose All the neighbours were looking. I'll never hear the end of it.
Mark Never mind, Mrs Hawkins. Try to look on the bright side, you've saved two p.
Gordon What's the idea, Padre? Chasing my mother down the road in her nightie? Been at the brandy again, have you?
Mark You're a fine one to talk. I don't get violent and attack my wife.
Rose No, you save that for your two fiancées.
Mark Two fiancées?
Gordon Does the vicar know you've got two fiancées?
Mark I haven't got two fiancées.
Gordon Ah, so he doesn't know!
Rose What's this? What's my bath towel doing here? It's sopping wet. Edward's been up to something in the bathroom.
Gordon Good heavens, he's not in there with Mother?
Rose (*at the bathroom door*) He'd better not be. Edward, come out of there.

Edward comes out of the main bedroom, very dishevelled, and with his shirt hanging out

Edward Yes, Rose? (*He stands very shame-faced*)

They all stare at him

Rose Edward!

Mrs Routledge comes out of the bathroom, and screams

Mrs Routledge How dare he try to frighten me! He's going to show everything.

Mrs Routledge runs into the spare room

Rose Mother, come back. There's nothing to be frightened of.
Gordon What are you doing with your shirt hanging out?
Edward The cat attacked me.
Rose We haven't got a cat.
Edward It was a stray cat.
Rose I'm not having any mangy, stray cats in my bedroom. I'll soon get rid of it. (*She goes towards the main bedroom door*)
Edward No, I've shoved him through the window, that's when he attacked me.
Mark Mrs Hawkins, I cannot understand why you seem to think that I have two fiancées?
Rose I don't think it, I know it. I've met them both.
Mark But you couldn't have. My fiancée hasn't arrived yet.

Act II

Rose Oh, so you've got another. That makes three.
Gordon The fellow's a drunken bigamist. Ought to be defrocked.
Rose Yes, and he will be as soon as I see the vicar in the morning.
Mark But Mrs Hawkins, it's all a terrible mistake.
Rose So you admit it. Too late to repent now.
Edward I don't think you should jump to conclusions, Rose.
Rose You leave him to me, Edward, I can deal with him.
Mark Don't you understand, that girl who was with me on the sofa, hadn't come to see me, she'd come to see Edward.
Rose A likely story.
Edward A likely story.
Rose Why should your fiancée want to see Edward?
Edward Yes, why should she want to see me?
Rose She was kissing *you*. She wasn't kissing Edward.
Edward She was kissing you, she wasn't kissing me.
Mark She said she wanted to get married and have lots of babies.
Rose That proves it. She can't have come to see Edward. I know he wouldn't do anything like that.
Gordon No point in going on, Rose. You won't get any sense out of the padre while he's on the bottle.
Mark *Me* on the bottle? I had to take your bottle away from you.
Gordon Yes, that's another thing. He's been stealing my brandy.
Mark I did it for your wife.
Gordon Now he's after my wife—mind you, he's welcome to her.
Mark I'm utterly confused. I think I must be going out of my mind.
Gordon It gets you like that.
Mark I shall go to the church and pray for spiritual guidance. God knows what's going on—at least I hope he does.

Mark goes out through the hall

Gordon I know why he's gone to the church—it's next door to the pub.
Rose This is the last time I shall take a curate into my house I can tell you. Bringing his fancy women in here. And where are they now, I should like to know?
Gordon Yes, where are they now?
Edward (*alarmed*) They've gone—hours ago.
Rose What do you know about it?
Edward Nothing.
Rose Be quiet then. Probably got them in his room.
Gordon Yes, with all that booze.
Edward No, they can't be in there, the door's still jammed. And they've all gone. He wouldn't dare keep them in here, not after you'd found out what I was up to—what he was up to.
Rose He's not getting up to it any more. He needn't think he's going to fill my house with girls.
Gordon Quite right, Rose. You'd think a man in his position would have more respect for the sanctity of married life.

Ingrid, Miss West Berlin, enters from the hall. She is tall, athletic, blonde and beautiful, in a Germanic way

Ingrid Gordon, I am cold sitting in your car, waiting for you.
Gordon (*acutely embarrassed*) Oh, Ingrid! Ah! Yes, Ingrid—er—Ingrid—well, Ingrid—you see, Ingrid—This is Ingrid.
Ingrid How do you do.
Gordon Oh—er—my little sister, Rose.
Rose How do you do.
Gordon Well, you see, little Ingrid—well, big Ingrid really—she's had a spot of bother. You see, she's Miss West Berlin.
Edward What!
Gordon I said she's Miss West Berlin.
Edward Oh my broken leg! (*He sits and holds a paper in front of his face*)
Gordon The idiots messed up the hotel accommodation. Put her in with Miss *East* Berlin. Poor little thing was terrified. Of course, I couldn't leave her there, so I've taken her under my wing.
Ingrid Yes, he is taking me to another hotel with him.
Gordon No, not with me, without me. I'm just dropping her off you understand.
Rose Very kind of you, Gordon, I must say.
Ingrid Yes, he knows of a little hotel, by the river, where they know him and the maids are very discreet.
Gordon (*acutely embarrassed*) Yes, it's run by two sweet old maids. They're very discreet and we don't want any diplomatic incidents, do we? Well, come along, my dear, the sweet old maids turn in very early.
Ingrid Yes I would like to go to bed early. Good-bye—Miss—er—Mrs ...
Rose Mrs Hawkins. Good-bye. (*He thumps Edward's paper*) Edward, say good-bye to Ingrid.
Edward (*mumbles*) Good-bye.
Ingrid Edward? Edward Hawkins?
Rose Yes, that's my husband. He works on the Telephone Exchange too. (*Aside to Edward*) Stand up, Edward, what's the matter with you?

Edward stands up, still holding the paper in front of his face. Rose snatches it away

You must excuse him. I think he's forgotten his manners.
Gordon Ignorant lout.
Ingrid But he has a lovely voice.
Gordon Well, come along, Ingrid, we must be off, before they lock up our hotel—your hotel.
Ingrid Oh! (*She staggers slightly*) Excuse me ... (*She sits*) I am so sorry, I am feeling faint.
Rose Oh you poor thing. You need medical attention. (*She goes to sideboard, gets the first-aid box*)
Gordon We'll call in at the doctor's on the way.
Rose He's no good. He'll make her worse. (*She offers smelling-salts*) You leave her to me, I'm fully qualified.

Act II

Edward But, Rose, you've only read the ...
Rose Do be quiet, Edward. (*To Ingrid*) Put your head between your knees.

Edward does so

   Not you, you silly boy.
Edward Oh, sorry dear.
Rose Don't just stand there, Gordon, get some water.
Gordon Water!

Gordon goes into the kitchen

Rose Feeling a little better, my dear?
Ingrid Thank you, yes. I feel a little better. I feel safe with you. You are a doctor?
Rose (*flattered*) Well no, not quite, but I have practised quite extensively.
Edward Yes, she's practised on her mother.
Rose Well she's still alive, isn't she?
Edward Yes nothing'll finish her off.
Ingrid You see, I have had nothing to eat all day.
Rose Good gracious. Disgraceful.

Gordon enters with a glass of water

Gordon Water.
Rose What are you giving her water for? She needs food. Look at her, she's half-starved.
Edward The other half isn't!
Rose You sit there. I'll make some nice sandwiches.
Gordon Well, hurry up then. We've got to get to the hotel.
Rose Hotel? She's not going to a nasty damp hotel by the river. She's staying here.
Edward What?!
Gordon What are you talking about? She doesn't want to stay here, do you?
Edward No, she doesn't want to stay here.
Rose Course she does. You would like to stay here, wouldn't you?
Ingrid Yes, I would like very much to stay here, please.
Edward (*desperately*) But we haven't got enough rooms. (*He looks round at them*)
Rose Nonsense. Mother can come in with me. Ingrid can have the spare room, and you, Edward, can have the Put-U-Up.
Edward I don't like sleeping on the Put-U-Up. I don't get any sleep.
Rose Course you will. Try counting sheep.

Rose goes off to the kitchen

Edward It's not sheep I'll be counting!
Ingrid Isn't it so kind of Mrs Hawkins to let me stay here?
Gordon } (*glumly*) Yes, very. { *Speaking*
Edward } { *together*

Edward sits on the Put-U-Up. Ingrid comes and sits beside Edward

Ingrid So, Mr Hawkins, you also work on the Telephone Exchange?
Edward Yes. (*He moves away slightly*)
Ingrid (*moving to him*) Perhaps we have spoken together?
Edward (*moving away*) Perhaps.
Ingrid One can make friends on the telephone. (*Moving to him*) Very good friends.

Edward gets up and moves away, sits in the armchair

Edward Can you? Yes I expect you can.

Gordon quickly sits on the other side of Ingrid

Gordon Yes, I've made some very good telephone friends myself, one way and another.
Ingrid Yes, I am sure. (*She gets up and sits on the arm of Edward's chair*) Tell me, Edward—I may call you Edward?
Edward (*lamely*) Yes.
Ingrid Tell me, what do you do in your spare time?
Edward I don't seem to be getting very much of that lately.
Ingrid I like to roller skate—you like to roller skate?
Gordon Roller skate? He couldn't roll a cigarette. (*He laughs*)
Ingrid (*ignoring Gordon*) Of course, it is much fun, but very dangerous. You can easily break a leg.
Edward Break a leg?
Ingrid I have an English friend who broke his leg. He told me on the telephone.
Edward Really.
Ingrid He was so brave.
Edward Was he really. (*He gets up*) I wonder if those sandwiches are ready.
Ingrid But it seems he made a wonderfully quick recovery. In no time he was jumping up and walking about.

Edward starts to affect a limp

Gordon Ingrid, are you quite sure you wouldn't like to stay in the comfortable luxury riverside hotel I've booked for you?
Edward Yes, it's lovely. Right on the river bank.
Ingrid I hate rivers.
Edward It's not all that near—in fact it's quite a long way back. It's not like being on a river at all.
Gordon The beds are very big and comfortable, so they tell me. Very popular place—full of life.
Ingrid Thank you. I do not like crowded hotels. It is so quiet here.
Edward Not for long it won't be.
Gordon As you don't like my arrangements, you might as well get your things out of my car.
Ingrid (*rising*) Of course. You are thoughtful to remind me. (*She goes to the hall door*)
Gordon I'll give you a hand. Of course you know, Ingrid, I've organized this Miss Europhone Contest almost single-handed.

Act II

Ingrid Perhaps you should have had help. I understand two of the girls are missing already.
Edward Are they really? Hadn't you better go and look for them, Gordon?
Gordon Don't you worry, they can't have gone far.

Gordon and Ingrid go out to the hall

Edward No, no, they haven't. They're here.

Edward dithers. He goes first to the main bedroom, then towards Mark's room, then towards the main bedroom again

Sylvana comes out of Mark's room just as Edward is about to open the main bedroom door

Sylvana Edward.
Edward Sssh! (*He runs to her*)
Sylvana Why do you leave me alone so long?
Edward One of the organizers is here, he mustn't see you. You will be disqualified from the Contest.
Sylvana Now I have found you I don't care about the Contest.
Edward But you must, for me. I want you to be Miss Europhone.
Sylvana I want to be Mrs London.
Edward You won't be Mrs anything, if they find you here. They'll send you back to Rome.
Sylvana Then we will be parted, dear.
Edward More like the dear departed, dear. Get back in there.
Sylvana But I am hungry.
Edward Food's on its way. In you go.

Edward bundles Sylvana into Mark's room. As Mark's door closes, Monique comes out of the main bedroom in her negligée

Edward reacts violently

Monique Edward.
Edward Aaaaah!
Monique It's very lonely in there.
Edward Well, it's not out here! I can't do anything like that. My wife's here. She'd kill me.
Monique Then you go and kill her first.
Edward Yes, I'll do it after supper.
Monique Supper—there is supper? I am starving.
Edward I'll bring you some. I hope she's made plenty of sandwiches.

The front door is heard opening

Gordon (*off*) After you, Ingrid.

Edward quickly bundles Monique into the main bedroom and shuts the door. As he moves down-stage the hall door opens, trapping him behind it, and Ingrid enters, carrying her coat and handbag, and a pair of roller-skates. Gordon follows, with her suitcase

Ingrid I think Edward is such a darling man, don't you? So witty and amusing.
Gordon Yes, a right clown. Oh, good he's gone. (*He closes the door and sees Edward*) What are you doing there, skulking behind the door?
Edward Nothing.
Gordon Well, go and do it somewhere else.
Edward I wish I could.

Gordon puts Ingrid's case down against the wall, above the hall door

Ingrid Edward, please do not go away. Come and sit with me. I love to hear your voice, it is so soothing.
Gordon Like cough drops.

The hall door is opened by Mark and conceals Gordon behind it. Mark is carrying the brandy bottle

Mark I feel better now. Oh no, not another one. I feel worse now. (*He shuts door and reveals Gordon*) Good gracious. What are you doing there? Hiding in shame, or looking for a bottle?
Gordon Don't need to look very far when you're around, do I? (*He grabs the bottle. He looks at it, sees that it is still full*) It's still full! What have you done—topped it up with water?
Mark (*to Ingrid*) It's a pity you're not topped up with water. Do forgive me, my dear, but he needs help. I don't think I've had the pleasure. You're not by any chance another fiancée of mine, are you? (*He laughs insanely*)
Gordon He's been at it again. Can't even remember how many fiancées he's got now.
Ingrid No, I am not your fiancée.
Mark Oh good, good. No offence, of course.
Edward This is Ingrid, she's staying the night.
Ingrid Yes, I am staying the night in the spare room.
Gordon Have a little drink, my dear.
Ingrid Oh, thank you.

Gordon goes to the sideboard to get glasses. Ingrid joins him

Mark Edward, I think you and I had better have a little talk. You must stop all this.
Edward I never meant it to start. It was only make-believe. I was having a lovely life till it turned up on my door step.
Mark Well you must get rid of it.
Edward I wish I could.
Mark You can if you try. But the flesh must be willing. Think of your wife. Send this poor girl home.
Edward Rose doesn't mind about her. She invited her to stay.
Mark Oh dear, things are worse than I thought. It's an orgy.

Rose comes in from the kitchen, pushing a trolley, on which is a plate full of sandwiches, coffee-pot and cups, etc.

Rose It's supper time. (*Frostily*) Oh, Mr Thomson, *you're* back.
Mark Yes, and none too soon, by the sound of things.

Act II

Ingrid Ah, sandwiches. Mrs Hawkins you are so kind. (*She sits on the Put-U-Up*)

Edward takes two sandwiches, one in each hand

Rose Edward! Manners, please.

Edward puts one sandwich back

Do help yourself, Ingrid. There's ham, cheese or bloater paste.
Ingrid Thank you. (*She takes one*)

Edward puts his sandwich in the first-aid box

Gordon (*to Mark*) I hate bloater. I've got my eye on that bottle, Padre.
Mark Mr Routledge. I implore you, give it up.
Gordon No, it's my brandy, you're not having it. (*He pours two drinks*)

Edward takes another sandwich

Rose Don't gobble, Edward, you'll get indigestion. (*She takes a sandwich*)
Gordon (*putting the drinks on the sofa table*) Well, if I'm not going to have my three-course dinner with champagne, I might as well have a cheese sandwich. (*He goes to the trolley and takes a sandwich*)

Mark takes Gordon's glass of brandy

Mark He must be saved. (*He drinks, and chokes*)

Gordon bites his sandwich. Edward puts his second sandwich in the first-aid box

Gordon Urgh! Bloater! Now where's my brandy? (*He goes back to his glass, finds it empty*) That's funny I thought I'd poured myself one. (*He goes to the sideboard and pours another*)

Edward goes to take another sandwich

Rose Haven't you had enough. You should leave some for others.
Edward (*desperately, pointing to the loggia*) It's that stray cat again, he can smell the bloater paste.
Rose (*running to the loggia*) Shoo, go away.

Ingrid turns to look at the loggia. Edward quickly puts the rest of the sandwiches in the first-aid box

What are you talking about, Edward? There's no cat there. (*She comes back*) Have another sandwich, Ingrid. (*She offers the plate, realizes it is empty*) Oh, well, I'm glad you've got a good appetite. Never mind, there's plenty more made in the kitchen. Gordon, would you mind, dear?
Gordon Why can't Edward get them?
Rose I don't trust him, he'll only eat them.
Gordon Yes, never knows when he's had enough.
Mark It's a pity *you* don't. (*He hiccups*) Pardon.

Gordon goes out to the kitchen

Rose starts to pour coffee. Mark picks up Gordon's glass of brandy

in the name of the Father, the Son and the Holy Ghost. Amen. (*He holds his nose and drinks, then puts the glass back*)

Gordon enters with a plate of sandwiches

Gordon Sandwiches. (*He puts them on the trolley*) Now where's my brandy? (*He picks up his empty glass*) Here, what's the game? There's something funny going on here. (*He looks hard at Mark, gets the bottle, pours a drink at the sofa table, puts bottle down in front of Mark*) Oh no, you don't. (*He takes the bottle back to the sideboard*)

Mark swigs the drink in one while Gordon's back is turned. Gordon comes back to his glass, finds it empty. Gordon bangs the glass down and glares at Mark, who starts to sway, giggle and hiccup

Gordon Have you been at my liquor, Vicar?
Mark I did it to save you from yourself, Mr Routledge.
Rose He's inebriated.
Gordon No he's not, he's blind drunk.
Mark (*singing*) "Stand up, stand up for Jesus" (*He falls unconscious behind the Put-U-Up*)
Gordon What did I tell you. Now perhaps I can have a drink. (*He pours one*)

Edward picks up the first-aid box, and goes towards the main bedroom. Rose turns and sees Edward

Rose Edward, where are you going with my first-aid box?
Edward Oh, er, I was just going to put it away. (*He goes towards sideboard*)
Rose Don't do that. Give it to me, I need it for Mr Thomson.
Edward No, best to leave him. There's nothing you can do for him.
Rose What do you know about it, you're not qualified, are you? Give me the box.
Edward But you said you didn't want anything more to do with him.
Rose That was when he was only a lodger, now he's a patient.
Edward But you're not in the medical profession.

Gordon puts his full glass down on the table

Gordon Oh, give her the box.
Rose (*taking the box*) Thank you. They'll soon bring him round, smelling salts. (*She opens the box*) Sandwiches! There's sandwiches in my bandages!
Gordon Do you always keep sandwiches in the first-aid box, Rose?
Rose Of course I don't. Edward, what are these sandwiches doing in here?
Edward Ah, er, they're for an emergency.
Rose What emergency?
Edward Famine relief.
Rose Don't talk nonsense. These are supposed to be sterile dressings. I shall have to throw the lot away now.
Edward Don't do that, I'll eat them.
Gordon That'll be nice, bloater and Dettol sandwiches.

Act II

Mark's hand comes up above the sofa table, takes the glass of brandy and disappears. They all stare transfixed. Ingrid squeals. Mark's hand replaces the now empty glass

Mark (*singing*) "Drink to me only with thine eyes." (*He snores*)
Gordon He's so far gone he even drinks in his sleep.

The telephone rings

Rose Answer it, will you, Gordon?

Rose takes the first-aid box into the kitchen

Gordon (*on the phone*) Hello ... Yes, Mr Routledge speaking ... What? Oh my God, this is terrible. I'll be right over. (*He puts the phone down*)

Rose comes back

Rose Who was it?
Gordon Andrews, my assistant organizer. Three of my girls are missing. They got off the plane but they never checked in at the hotel.
Edward No, no, it's only two. I mean, you said it's only two.
Gordon It was two, but now it's three. Miss Paris, Miss Rome and now Miss Oslo.
Edward Oh no, not Snowdrop!
Gordon Snowdrop?
Edward Yes, the snow drops a lot in Oslo. It's in Norway you know.
Gordon I know Oslo's in Norway, but where's Miss Oslo? She's on the loose in West London. Right. You come with me, Edward, make yourself useful for a change.
Edward But I can't go. I've got to help Rose. She needs me, don't you, Rose.
Rose What for?
Edward Well, to do the washing up.
Rose Don't be silly, I'll do that. Anyway, Ingrid will help me, won't you, my dear?
Ingrid Of course, I will be most happy, Mrs Hawkins.
Edward But ...
Rose Go along and help Gordon find his girls.
Gordon If we don't find them soon, I shall have to inform the police.
Edward Police! We don't want to bother them. I'll come with you.
Gordon Don't wait up, we might be all night.

Gordon goes out of the hall door

Edward We might even be longer.

Edward follows Gordon off

Rose It's not like Gordon, he never loses things. I'd understand if it was Edward, he's very absent-minded. (*She takes the trolley towards the kitchen*)
Ingrid Yes, I think his mind is often on other things. (*Indicating Mark*) What shall we do with the drunken preacher?

Rose (*singing*) "What shall we do with the drunken preacher?" (*She laughs*) Leave him where he is. I'll deal with him later.

Rose and Ingrid go into the kitchen

Mark slowly rises from behind the Put-U-Up. He heaves himself on to his feet, sways

Mark I think I'd better go to bed. "Lord now lettest thou thy servant depart in peace."

Mark walks uncertainly to the main bedroom, goes in closing the door behind him. There is a squeal from Monique. Mark comes out

I beg your pardon, Madam. Wrong room. (*He shuts the door and realizes what he has seen*)

Mark staggers towards his own door, goes in. There is a torrent of Italian abuse. The door opens again and Mark staggers out, with a tennis racket around his neck. He closes the door

I beg your pardon, Signora. (*He realizes who is in his room*) Good gracious, it's the lady with the babies. (*Now he is pleased with himself—thinks he's going to crack the problem. He backs to the kitchen door, keeping his eyes on his bedroom door all the time*) Mrs Hawkins ...

Mark hurries into the kitchen. As the kitchen door closes, Mark's bedroom door opens, Sylvana, in a dressing-gown, comes out and goes into the bathroom. As that door closes, Rose, in an apron, Mark, still with the tennis racket on, and Ingrid, with a tea towel, come out of the kitchen

I wish to clear up this misunderstanding once and for all, Mrs Hawkins, she is not an hallucination. She is real flesh and blood. Certainly plenty of flesh.
Rose I'm getting very tired of this tomfoolery. Who do you think you've seen?
Mark The one—the one, who's my fiancée, only she isn't my fiancée, she's the other one.
Rose I don't believe a word of it.

Rose goes into Mark's room

Mark Watch out for her overhead smash.

Rose comes out of Mark's room

Rose Just as I thought. You *have* got the D.T.'s. Get into your room and stay there.
Mark My room and stay there.
Rose When you've slept off the drink, you can pack your bags and go.

Rose goes into the kitchen

Ingrid (*removing tennis racket and putting it in his hand*) It's a good thing she plays tennis, not base-ball!

Ingrid goes into the kitchen

Act II

Mark looks at the tennis racket. He grins through the frame

Mark I must be seeing things. Anyone for hallucinations?

Mark staggers into his room and closes the door. Edward appears at the french windows. He looks round to see if the coast is clear, then comes in. He starts towards the main bedroom. After a moment Mark comes in from his room, without tennis racket, he sees Edward

Ah! Are you an hallucination or are you real?

Edward What were you doing in there?

Mark It's my room.

Edward Did you see anyone in there?

Mark Oh yes—lady with a tennis racket. But she's gone now. And the other one too.

Edward What other one?

Mark The one in there—(*he indicates main bedroom*)—with her nightie on. But she isn't there now. She's gone. They've all gone away.

Edward All gone? Thank goodness for that.

Mark It's the brandy, you know. They were never there at all—just hallucinations.

Edward Brandy? Good idea, I could do with one. (*He pours himself a stiff brandy and puts the bottle down*)

Mark Oh dear, have I got to save you too. (*He picks up the glass*) Amen! (*He drinks the brandy down in one, holds on to the glass, totters to the Put-U-Up, and sits*)

Edward Don't worry, I'll save myself.

Mark Thank goodness for that.

Edward is about to pour another drink. He gets another glass from the sideboard, which he holds on to. He sits beside Mark and pours them each a drink

Edward No wonder you've been seeing things. This stuff's strong enough to give you spots before the eyes.

Mark No, not spots—girls. Lovely girls. I'm so sorry they've gone.

Edward I'm not. Here have another one. (*He pours more brandy*)

Mark Thanks I will—perhaps they'll come back again.

They drink

Sylvana comes out of the bathroom

Mark sees her first

It's working! One of them has!

Edward What are you talking about? (*He turns and sees Sylvana. He tries to get up, unsuccessfully*) Oh my God!

Sylvana So there you are. Now I know why you do not come to me. You are drunk. *Stupido.*

Sylvana flounces into Mark's bedroom

Edward I've got to do something about her.

Mark You've already done it. You've made her disappear again.
Edward If she's here, the other one must be. (*He moves to the main bedroom*)
Mark (*taking another drink*) Let's have another drink. That'll make her come back.

Edward opens the main bedroom door

Monique comes out

Monique Edward, where have you been?
Mark It's marvellous stuff this brandy! There's a girl in every glass!
Edward You'll have to go—you can't stay here.
Monique I want to be with you.
Edward I'll join you later.
Monique But where shall I go?
Edward Go to a secret meeting place.
Monique Where is that?
Edward How should I know? It's secret, isn't it? But wherever it is, you must go.
Mark Leave her to me. I'll get rid of her. I'll exorcize her. (*He gets up*)
Edward Good idea. You exercise her round the garden for a bit, while I think of something.
Monique You will think of a meeting place?
Edward Yes, I've thought of it. There's a nice little greenhouse in the garden. I'll come to you there.
Monique I will wait for you.

Mark takes Monique by the arm and steers her towards the french windows

Mark You don't feel ephemeral? Never mind. By bell, book and candle I command you to return from whence you came. And you can take me with you.

Mark and Monique go out to the garden

Edward takes another swig of brandy

Rose comes in from the kitchen, followed by Ingrid

Edward reacts

Edward Blimey, there were two in that glass.
Rose Did you and Gordon find those girls?
Edward Yes and no.
Rose What do you mean, yes and no?
Edward Yes I did and no Gordon didn't. Anyway it's all being sorted out now—I hope.
Rose I'm going to settle Mother in my room, then we can all go to bed.
Ingrid Yes, that is what I have been waiting for.
Rose Edward, make up the Put-U-Up for yourself. Ingrid'll help you. She's been such a help to me.
Ingrid Yes, I would like to help you with the Put-U-Up, Edward.
Edward It's all right, I can manage on my own.

Act II

Ingrid It is much better with two. I know all about these things.
Edward I was afraid you might.
Rose That's the way, Ingrid. You show him how to do it.

Rose goes into the spare room

Ingrid *Ja*, I will. At last we are alone.
Edward So we are.
Ingrid Do you not think I have been clever?
Edward Clever?

They open the Put-U-Up. The bedclothes are inside

Ingrid I am nice to your wife, now she is putty in my hands. She sleeps with her mother, she gives me the spare room and you can come to me. It is most exciting, *ja*?
Edward Thrilling!

Rose and Mrs Routledge come out of the spare room

Mrs Routledge I absolutely refuse to change rooms. I've only just managed to get myself warm. This house is like an ice box.
Rose Well, you've got your hot-water bottle, Mother.
Mrs Routledge It's useless. It's stone cold.
Rose I'll put the kettle on for another one.
Ingrid No, please, Mrs Hawkins, allow me. I would like to do it for your old *mutter*.

Ingrid goes into the kitchen

Mrs Routledge Who's she calling an old nutter? And who is she? I've never seen her before.
Rose She's a very nice German girl. She's on the telephones, like Edward. She's staying the night.
Mrs Routledge Well I'm certainly not giving up my room for one of his frightful friends.
Edward She's a friend of Gordon's.
Mrs Routledge Oh, that's quite different. You're very welcome, my dear. Any friend of Gordon's ...
Rose That's right, Mother. Let's get you to sleep.

Rose ushers Mrs Routledge into the main bedroom

(*To Edward*) Hurry up with that bed. As soon as I've got Mother settled I'd better have a look at Mr Thomson. After all, he is a patient, I suppose.

Rose goes into the main bedroom

Edward Oh no. Now I'll have to move the spaghetti queen. (*He goes into Mark's room*) Come on quick, out of here, you'll have to move. (*He comes out with a bundle of clothes and case*)

Sylvana follows Edward

Sylvana What are you doing? I do not want to move.

Edward Well, you'll have to. Anyway this is a much nicer room, it faces Naples. (*He opens spare room door and goes in*)
Sylvana Napoli? I do not like Napoli.
Edward (*coming out*) Well, keep the curtains closed and you won't notice.

Edward pushes Sylvana into the spare room and shuts the door. Rose comes out of the main bedroom

Rose Good night, Mother. (*She shuts the door*) I've sedated her. Put her out for the night.
Edward She ought to be put down.
Rose What did you say, dear?
Edward I said the Put-U-Up's put down.
Rose Well, don't hang about then, get into bed. I'll just take a look at my alcoholic patient. (*She goes into Mark's room, and comes out immediately*) He's escaped. Where's he gone?
Edward How should I know.
Rose Well, I wash my hands of him. Probably get arrested. Serve him right.

Ingrid comes out with the hot-water bottle

Ingrid This is lovely and hot.
Rose Thank you, dear. Mother will be most grateful to you. I'll be off to bed now. You know where you're sleeping?
Ingrid Yes, I know. Good night, Mrs Hawkins.
Rose Good night.

Rose goes into the main bedroom

Ingrid This is spicy, *ja*? I will undress and you will join me. (*She takes her case and goes towards the spare room*)
Edward No, not in there, over here.
Ingrid But this is my room.
Edward No, not any longer. This room. Change of plan. I've just remembered, the wall's very thin in there.
Ingrid Ah, so you are a noisy lover? Good.

Ingrid slaps Edward on the back and goes into Mark's room

Edward She'll have to go, that one.

Edward takes off his trousers, then his tie, and starts to get into bed

Mark comes in through the french windows

Mark Come back, spirit. I haven't finished exorcizing you yet. She's gone. It must have worked. I must tell the Bishop. (*He comes face to face with Edward*) Ah! There you are, Edward. I found myself wandering about alone in the garden by the greenhouse.
Edward Alone?
Mark But I have a vague recollection that there was somebody with me.
Edward No, no. That was one of your hallucinations.
Mark Have I been having hallucinations?

Act II 53

Edward Yes, you'd better go to bed. You'll feel better in the morning.
Mark Yes, I think I should. (*He goes towards his room, picking up his night things*) Nightie-nightie.
Edward No, you can't go in there.
Mark Can't I?
Edward No, the door's jammed. It's the house. It's started to subside again.
Mark Thank goodness for that, I thought it was me.
Edward You'll have to spend the night in—(*he looks at each door in turn*)—in the Put-U-Up with me.
Mark Oh, I see. Needs must when the devil drives. And he'll have to, I don't want to get breathalized. What a bit of luck I've got my night things out. I'll just put them on. Excuse me. (*He starts to undress, thinks better of it*) On second thoughts I think I'll go in the bathroom and do it. I've just remembered that vicar in the vestry in Wimbledon.

Mark goes into the bathroom

Edward has some difficulty getting into bed, but eventually he turns out the lights and settles down, starting to go to sleep

After a moment, Monique comes in from the garden: she looks around, sees Edward, and calls quietly

Monique Edward, Edward.

No reply, only a snore

Quelle affaire! (*She gets into bed*)

Edward is on one side of the bed, Monique is in the centre. She snuggles under the clothes

Mark comes in from the bathroom in his pyjamas

Mark gets into bed. He is yawning, almost asleep. He lies down. Suddenly he sits up and gets out of bed. He kneels down at the foot of the bed and says a quick silent prayer. He gets into bed again, and lies down. There is a snore from Edward. Then a snore from Mark. Monique sits up, looks from one to the other. She smiles

Ah, la ménage à trois. Formidable! (*She snuggles down between them*)

After a moment, Gordon creeps in through the french windows and tiptoes down to the spare room

Gordon My little drop of German mustard.

Gordon goes into the spare room, closing the door quietly behind him

There is a moment's pause, then a scream, a crash. Edward and Mark sit up in bed

Gordon staggers out with a toy fort over his head. A torrent of Italian abuse comes from inside

I beg your pardon, Madam—wrong room.

Sylvana, still shouting in Italian, comes out, leaving the door open, and pushes Gordon through the french windows

Edward What's Gordon up to?
Mark What's going on, Edward?
Monique (*sitting up*) What is happening?

Mark and Edward react. They leap out of bed. Edward turns on the lights. Their pyjama trousers fall down. Monique holds up the two pyjama cords she has removed in the bed

Mark I'm seeing things again.

Mark dashes into the bathroom

Edward has a tug of war with the sheet. Tears it, and uses it as a loin-cloth. The main bedroom opens—Rose speaks, off

Rose (*off*) Edward, what's all that noise?
Edward My wife! Quick, get under the sheet.

Monique dives under the bedclothes

Rose enters, doing up her dressing-gown

Rose What are you doing, Edward?
Edward I fell out of bed. (*He has difficulties with his "loin-cloth"*)

Ingrid comes out of Mark's room

Ingrid Is someone playing night games?
Rose Ingrid. What are you doing in there? That's Mr Thomson's room.
Ingrid Edward made me go in there.
Rose Edward, did you tell her to go in with Mr Thomson?
Edward Course I didn't. He's gone out. (*He has more trouble with the sheet*)
Rose What happens when he comes back? Why didn't you put her in the spare room as I told you?
Edward The door's stuck.
Rose Nonsense, it's wide open.
Edward It must have come unstuck.
Rose I must apologize for my husband, Ingrid. He doesn't seem to know what he's doing.
Ingrid Please don't apologize. I think he knows what he is doing. He's just trying to be helpful.

Ingrid eyes Edward. He is embarrassed

Rose You go into the spare room, you won't be disturbed again.
Ingrid I do not mind being disturbed, thank you, Mrs Hawkins.

Ingrid goes into the spare room and closes the door

Rose Now then, Edward, get back into bed.
Edward (*reacting*) Yes, I will.
Rose Go on, then.

Act II   55

Edward What, now?
Rose Will you get back into bed?
Edward Yes, Rose. (*He sits on top of the blankets*)
Rose Inside, properly.
Edward I feel hot.
Rose Of course, you've got a temperature. Under the blankets at once.
Edward Yes, Rose.

Edward gingerly creeps into the very edge of the bed

Rose That's better. Lie down properly.

He starts to slide down. Rose turns to go. Edward lets out a cry. Rose looks back

What's the matter?
Edward She's cold—the sheet's cold!
Rose You'll soon warm up.
Edward That's what I'm afraid of.
Rose Lie down and go to sleep.

Rose goes into the main bedroom and closes the door

Edward leaps out of bed. Monique sits up

Monique Who was that Ingrid girl?
Edward Ingrid girl? Just a friend of my wife's. You have to go. It's not safe for you to stay a minute longer.
Monique But I cannot go. I have no clothes.
Edward Well, get them.
Monique Very well.
Edward Where are they?
Monique In there. (*She indicates the main bedroom*)
Edward No! You can't go in there.
Monique Then I cannot go.
Edward Oh, it's too much, things are getting too hot.
Monique It was too hot under the blankets. I must have water. And I am hungry. As nobody gives me anything, I will make myself an omelet.

Monique goes into the kitchen

Edward goes to follow her

Sylvana comes running in through the french windows

Sylvana That horrible man. He is trying to take my honour. I chase him round and round but I do not catch him.
Edward Quick, go back in there. (*He indicates spare room*)
Sylvana I will not go back in that room. He may return.
Edward Quite right. Don't go in there, go in there. (*He indicates Mark's room*) He won't find you in there.
Sylvana For this my brothers would kill him. (*She gestures slitting her throat*) But they are not here.

Edward Just as well by the sound of it.
Sylvana But I am betrothed to you, so you must kill him. (*She repeats the throat-slitting gesture*)
Edward I've always wanted to. But I'd never get away with it.
Sylvana If you do not kill him, my brothers will kill you.

Sylvana goes into Mark's bedroom, shutting the door

Edward is very nervous

Monique pokes her head out of the kitchen, with a frying-pan in her hand

Monique I can only find ten eggs.

Monique goes back into the kitchen

Edward Ssh, or we'll all be in the frying pan.

Edward follows Monique into the kitchen. Mark comes out of the bathroom. He wears a lavatory chain round his pyjama trousers to keep them up. He looks round, yawns, gets into bed, pulls the blankets over his head and goes to sleep. Gordon creeps in from french windows, looks around, tiptoes to door of Mark's room

Gordon Now my little Rhine maiden.

Gordon goes into Mark's room and shuts the door. There is a moment's pause, then a scream, a crash, and a torrent of Italian abuse. Gordon comes staggering out pursued by Sylvana, who is trying to swat him with a pillow. Edward comes running out of the kitchen. She connects with Edward by mistake, the pillow bursts in a shower of feathers. Gordon runs off through the hall, followed by Sylvana.

Rose (*off*) Edward! Edward!

Edward runs off into the kitchen. Rose enters

Edward, there's feathers everywhere. Who's had a bird in here? Edward, wake up. (*She shakes Mark, who sits up*)
Mark I'm seeing things again. I'm having nightmares now.
Rose What are you doing there?
Mark Sleeping.
Rose Where's my Edward? What have you done with him?

Gordon pursued by Sylvana, runs in through french windows and out through the hall

Gordon You don't understand. I haven't got my phrase book.
Rose Gordon, what are you doing? Gordon, come back. (*Rose runs off after Gordon and Ingrid*)
Mark Don't go near him, he's mad with drink. Come back, you Gadarene swine.

Mark runs off after Rose. Edward peeps out of kitchen, looks round, goes to his trousers, gets them half on. Monique comes out of the kitchen.

Act II

Monique Edward ...

The swing door hits Edward in the behind, and he goes sprawling

Your omelet's ready.

Shouting is heard from Sylvana, Gordon, Rose and Mark, outside in the garden

Edward They're coming back. (*He runs below the Put-U-Up*) Hide!

Monique runs into the kitchen. Ingrid shoots out of the spare room on roller skates

Ingrid Edward! Liebchen! (*She skates across towards Edward*)

Edward runs above the Put-U-Up, then round the room to below it, then dives into it. It folds up on top of him; he disappears inside it. It now looks like a sofa. N.B. This is a trick bed. As he runs, Ingrid skates round, following him

As Edward lands in the Put-U-Up Ingrid skates off into the spare room, and the door shuts. Gordon and Sylvana run on through the french windows. Gordon runs off and out of the front door. Sylvana stops in the middle of the room

Sylvana Go away. If you come back I will kill you.

Sylvana goes into Mark's room and slams the door. Mark runs on. Monique comes out of the kitchen

Monique Please tell me, what is happening. (*She puts the omelet pan on the armchair*)

Mark I don't know. I think they're all possessed. Oh, my head. (*He sits on the Put-U-Up*)

There is a cry from Edward

Monique It is bad? (*She sits beside him*)

Another cry from Edward

It sounds very bad.
Mark Yes it is.
Monique You should have some black coffee. (*She rises*)
Mark (*rising*) No, no. I'll make it. You sit down.

She sits. Another cry from Edward

Oh, have you got it too? I'll bring you a cup.

Mark goes into the kitchen

Edward's arm comes out of the end of the Put-U-Up. It waves about. Monique sees it, screams, jumps up. Edward opens up the bed

Monique Oh, my poor Edward, you are squashed.
Edward Now I know what pressed beef feels like. Help me up. (*He has one leg doubled up under him*) My leg! Where's my leg?

Monique tries to pull him up, over-balances, and falls on top of him

Rose comes on through french windows

Rose Edward!

Edward and Monique get up

Mrs Routledge enters from the bedroom, brandishing an umbrella

Mrs Routledge What is going on in here?
Rose Edward, what are you doing in bed with that woman?
Monique *Excusez-moi.*

Monique runs off to the kitchen

Mrs Routledge You beast! You swine! How dare you treat me and my daughter like this. You're evil.
Edward No, no. You don't understand. I haven't done anything.
Rose No, you haven't had the chance. Filling my house with your foreign tarts.
Mrs Routledge He ought to be doctored.
Edward Will you shut up, you interfering old bag.
Mrs Routledge Oh! (*She sinks into the chair, sits on the omelet*)
Rose Don't you speak to my mother like that. Look what you've done to her, you've brought on her palpitations.
Edward Good.
Mrs Routledge My bottom's burning! (*She gets up, finds omelet stuck to her*)
Rose You sadist. You've burnt Mother's bottom.
Edward That's not the only thing I'd like to do to her.

Ingrid's door opens. Gordon emerges, propelled out by Ingrid, who has him in an arm-lock. She is not wearing roller skates

Ingrid How dare you climb in my window.
Rose Gordon!
Gordon I can explain.
Ingrid He tried to assault me in my bed. He is after all the girls. He is sex crazy gorilla. We're defenceless.

Ingrid marches Gordon off, protesting, to the hall

Rose What's Gordon been doing?
Edward What she said. Attacking her. And the other two as well.
Rose But what are they all doing here?
Edward Gordon brought them here. He made me hide them.
Rose Who are they?
Edward The Miss Europhone girls. Miss Paris, Miss Rome and Miss West Berlin. Why do you think Gordon got himself on the committee?
Rose Oh, Edward, how I've misjudged you. How can you ever forgive me?
Edward Perhaps I won't.
Mrs Routledge I don't believe a word of it. He's telling lies about my Gordon.
Rose Oh, shut up, you interfering old bag!
Mrs Routledge What?!

Act II

Rose You've always tried to come between me and Edward. You've never liked my Edward.
Mrs Routledge Oh, you've made my palpitations worse.
Rose You haven't got any. There's nothing the matter with you, there never has been. You're as strong as an ox.
Edward Yes, and as stupid as a cow.
Mrs Routledge Oh!
Rose (*pleased*) Oh Edward, that's the nicest thing you've ever said.

Edward takes Rose's hand, and they go towards the main bedroom

Miss Oslo enters from the hall, dressed in furs

Miss Oslo Excuse me, do I have the right house?
Edward Who are you?
Miss Oslo I am Britt—Miss Oslo.
Edward My God, Snowdrop!
Miss Oslo *Ja.* Is this the house of Mr Edward Hawkins?
Rose Yes, that's right.
Edward No, no it's not. I'm not—er—he's not here.
Rose Edward, who is this girl?
Miss Oslo Edward? Then you are him. You are my darling Mr London. (*She runs to him*)
Mrs Routledge He's got another one. I'll soon stop him.

Mrs Routledge grabs an old musket off the wall, it goes off with a loud report. Pandemonium. The chandelier comes shooting down. Edward runs to it and hangs on as the chandelier flies up to the ceiling and through it, taking Edward with it, amidst a shower of plaster, etc.

Monique, Mark, Sylvana and Ingrid appear at various doors, as—

the CURTAIN *falls*

FURNITURE AND PROPERTY LIST

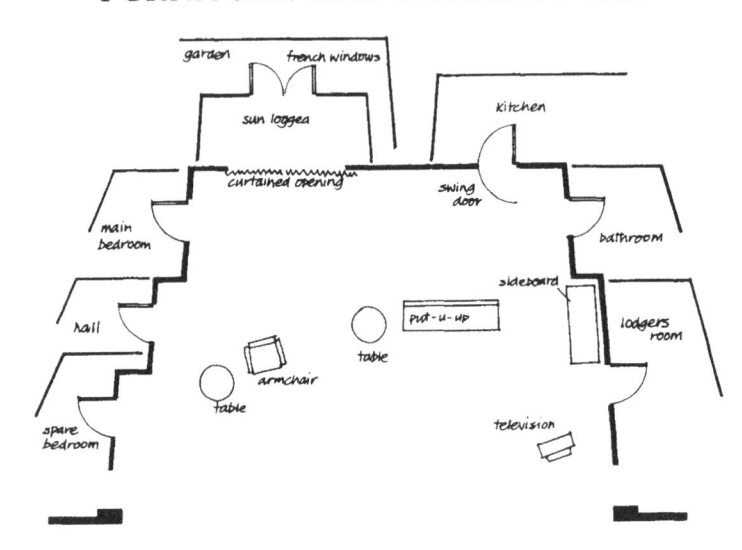

ACT I

On stage: Put-U-Up. *On it:* cushions, newspaper. *In it:* bedclothes
Armchair. *On it:* cushions, **Rose's** handbag
T.V. set. *On top:* letter
Occasional table by Put-U-Up
Occasional table by armchair
Sideboard. *On it:* telephone, ashtray. *In cupboards:* sherry, beer, assorted glasses, one broken glass, pieces of glass for crash, first-aid box with various medicaments including bottle of smelling salts. *Beside it:* wastepaper basket
Around walls: various war relics, including old musket (fireable)
In bathroom door: key

Off stage: Front door with practical knocker and slam
Duster **(Rose)**
Wrapped box of toy soldiers on green board **(Edward)**
Shopping basket with various foodstuffs **(Rose)**
Spongebag **(Rose)**
Bunch of flowers, books **(Mark)**
Small suitcase **(Monique)**
Bottle of brandy **(Monique)**
2 ledgers **(Mark)**

Furniture and Property List 61

    Vase for flowers **(Mark)**
    Sack of potatoes **(Edward)**
    Briefcase **(Gordon)**
    Account book **(Mark)**
    2 suitcases **(Gordon)**
    Tray with 2 cups of tea, 2 saucers, 2 teaspoons **(Rose)**
    Lavatory seat **(Edward)**
    Green ledger **(Edward)**
    Hot-water bottle **(Rose)**
    Broken mug handle **(Edward)**
    Tea trolley with packet of tea, packet of sugar, half-full bottle of milk, teapot, kettle with water, several odd cups in disorder **(Edward)**
    Bed sheets **(Rose)**
    Night things **(Mark)**

Personal: **Gordon:** cigarettes in case, lighter, concert tickets
    Mark: bicycle clips
    Monique: perfume spray in handbag

ACT II

Off stage: Towel **(Monique)**
    Glass of water **(Gordon)**
    Roller skates, handbag **(Ingrid)**
    Suitcase **(Gordon)**
    Trolley with plate of sandwiches, coffee pot, 5 cups, saucers, spoons, cream jug, sugar bowl **(Rose)**
    Plate of sandwiches **(Gordon)**
    Broken tennis racket **(Mark)**
    Tea towel **(Ingrid)**
    Hot-water bottle **(Ingrid)**
    Apron **(Rose)**
    Broken toy fort **(Gordon)**
    Frying pan **(Monique)**
    Lavatory chain **(Mark)**
    Pillow **(Sylvana)**
    Umbrella **(Mrs Routledge)**

Personal: **Mark:** diary

LIGHTING PLOT

Property fittings required: counter-weighted adjustable chandelier (unlit, but strong enough to bear man's weight), wall brackets

Interior. A living-room. The same scene throughout

ACT I   Early evening

To open: Wall brackets on. General effect of early evening light outside windows

Cue 1:   As CURTAIN rises   (Page 1)
Start slow fade to dusk outside windows

ACT II   Evening

To open: As close of Act I

Cue 2:   **Edward** switches off lights   (Page 53)
Snap off wall brackets, retaining faint evening glow

Cue 2:   **Edward** switches on lights   (Page 54)
Return to previous lighting

EFFECTS PLOT

ACT I

Cue 1:	**Rose** plumps up cushion *Telephone rings*	(Page 3)
Cue 2:	**Edward:** "... but I mustn't." *Telephone rings*	(Page 16)
Cue 3:	**Edward** exits to kitchen *Crockery crash*	(Page 30)

ACT II

Cue 4:	**Edward:** "... what an idea." *Sound of running tap water*	(Page 37)
Cue 5:	**Edward:** "... bathing in it." *Loud water splash*	(Page 37)
Cue 6:	**Gordon:** "... drinks in his sleep." *Telephone rings*	(Page 47)